The Adult Attachment Workbook

Powerful Strategies to Promote
Understanding, Increase Security,
and Build Long-Lasting
Relationships

Kate Homily

from various sources. Please consult a licensed professional before attempting any techniques outlined in this book.

By reading this document, the reader agrees that under no circumstances is the author responsible for any losses, direct or indirect, that are incurred as a result of the use of the information contained within this document, including, but not limited to, errors, omissions, or inaccuracies.

Table of Contents

Introduction

"It's all about falling in love with yourself and sharing that love with someone who appreciates you, rather than looking for love to compensate for a self love deficit."

~ Eartha Kitt

You've done it again. You entered another relationship that seemed destined to fail. This has become your modus operandi, or so it seems. Why do you go for a certain type of person? It almost seems to be your weakness. However, this is not your weakness; instead, it is your own style of attachment.

From your primary relationship, your bond with your childhood caregivers, you have learned to behave in a certain way. This type of behavior has become a habit that is ingrained in your thinking and doing. These behaviors are known as styles of attachment. Psychologists have conducted many tests and research studies over the years to discover why people do things the way they do them, and John Bowlby (a psychoanalyst) finally created the theory of attachments to explain the four styles of attachment that were identified.

In a nutshell, the best form of attachment that is most stable and responsive to change and helps you to be in a successful relationship is known as a secure attachment style. This style of attachment usually develops in children who are raised in homes with dependable parents who quickly address their children's fears and help them deal with stressors in a responsible manner. In essence, these children grow up to be secure self-loving adults, and this enables them to share that love with others in a responsible and compassionate way.

The three other styles of attachment are known as insecure attachment styles and start in children who are raised in homes where there was irregular activity, with parents who were not dependable and emotionally unavailable, where they suffered trauma and neglect. These styles all enable us to deal with the stressors of a relationship in different ways, and because of them, we can engage in harmful behavior. There is also evidence of insecure attachment styles contributing to mental health challenges as people struggle to deal with trauma or to build their self-confidence, and we should all try to move towards more secure attachment styles.

If you find yourself displaying the characteristics of any of these three attachment styles, you tend to engage in self-sabotaging behavior in your relationships. You are drawn to the wrong partners, or even when you have an ideal partner, you tend to mess things up or leave that partner. So, how do you get to a point where you can enter a healthy relationship, or even create your own happiness without being in a relationship or partnership? Certainly, you do not need to be a victim of your past.

By dealing with your attachment issues, you will enrich your long-term relationships and heal the broken connections within yourself and between other people in your life. You need to return to a sense of wholeness, the original trusting and caring person you were before you were robbed of your potential by trauma. And, even if that trauma originated in your childhood, it can impact your life today, creating dissociation and a loss of boundaries.

This book is about reclaiming your birthright, finding healthy connections and redeveloping compassion with yourself and with others. By becoming aware of your behavioral mechanisms and attachment behaviors, you will start to see why you make certain decisions, replace your fear with curiosity, and connect with your peers as you enter into healthy relationships with yourself and with others.

In these pages, you will get a better understanding of attachment theory as it applies in your life and the life of your partner. You will come to understand different approaches to interventions as you learn to form deeper bonds, develop your self-confidence, and learn to trust. Looking at all the relationships in your life, whether platonic, romantic, or familial, you will learn a variety of therapeutic techniques and approaches to help you develop a secure attachment style and heal your core wounds.

Your adult behavior need not be a continued reflection of your childhood traumas, and a deep personal transformation is possible. There are a range of traditional psychological methods and new cutting-edge technologies available to help with your transformation. Change is powerful, and you can build more secure and lasting relationships with the people in your life, especially with the people you care about most. Let me be your guide, your therapist, and your compass.

My name is Kate Homily, and I have been a relationship therapist for 18 years. Throughout my long years of family practice, I have seen and even experienced many forms of relationship anxiety myself. I have successfully helped all my clients overcome their own unique relationship challenges by identifying their attachment styles, exploring how this affects their lives and relationships, and planning a constructive guided path for them to work through to achieve their own relationship goals and find happiness. In this book, I hope to share the wisdom and experience I have amassed in my years of helping people of all ages, genders, and races.

I have applied my theories and experience to my own life with great success. Many years ago, I also experienced relationship anxiety, and the battle I won has shaped my approach to relationship therapy to a large extent. Today, I am a happily married mother, and I have built a harmonious life with my family, my two kids, and also my two rambunctious puppies. I no longer spend my days worrying about the what-ifs or that my life could fall apart. Through my experiences, my training, and my years of helping my clients, I have discovered how to enjoy all of my blessings and practice gratitude everyday.

Starting today, you can also develop strategies to strengthen your romantic relationships, understand yourself better, and be a better version of your authentic self with the people you care about. Blessings and daily gratitude is within your reach as you learn to let go of anxieties, create coping strategies, and improve your behavior to become the best version of yourself today. Let go of reacting out of harmful instincts and develop the ability to act with control and compassion right now.

Chapter 1:

Attachment Styles: Where Do You Fall on the Spectrum?

Image 1: Geralt on Pixabay. None of us live in isolation. We connect with and to other people, places, and even things. This great big network affects our psyche, and if we are not consciously aware of it and learn to effectively manage it, we can end up being

tangled up in it and losing our ability to determine our life course. We react instead of mindfully acting.

Attachment: A Brief History

Attachments form in your early childhood. Before you can even speak or even before your conscious memories form, you start interacting with the people around you. From your first wail, you are engaging in behavior to find the best way to navigate your life. If you were fortunate enough to have responsive parents or primary caregivers who rapidly soothed your wails, fed you on time, eased you from any discomfort, ensured you had routines to develop trust, and kept you healthy from childhood illnesses, you will most likely have developed a secure attachment style. You have been conditioned to believe in the world around you as being good and predictable, which created a low level of anxiety in you.

This will, in turn, create healthy brain chemistry as your body develops naturally. However, should you have been raised in a home that was unpredictable or traumatic, you will have developed a completely different style of attachment. You have been exposed to loud noises, tensions, irregular feeding, lack of comfort, increased levels of fear, and start to develop trust issues. This will result in you forming harmful attachment behavior.

With young children, this is known as reactive attachment disorder. You learn to react to a situation in a negative or harmful way, based on the childhood traumas that shaped your instincts. Later, as an adult, this has created a harmful behavior and thinking paradigm. Your distrustful and self-protecting behaviors have become your personality. As a result, you may have become abusive, or seek abusers, you may have become avoidant, or distrust people, or feel ambivalence that keeps you from making any real connection to other people. In relationships, this causes breakups, conflict, and further trauma.

Image 2: Kelly Sikkema on Unsplash. Attachment styles are about more than just romantic attachments; they are about how you share yourself with the world as you understand it. Your worldview is created by how you see the people, places, and events around you. This, in turn, determines how you respond to that world.

There are four distinctive attachment styles, and you could lean towards any of them, depending on your behavior. It is important to find out what triggers you and then work towards a strategy for coping with your past traumas so you can feel more secure and involved in your relationships. You can create a healthy attachment in your relationships, and this includes your relationship with yourself. Here is a brief overview of the four attachment styles to consider:

The Four Attachment Styles

- **Secure Attachment Style**

A child who sees their parents and experiences positive emotions will likely smile and appear happy. They are content to greet their parents and also to say farewell to their parents, and they are secure in the knowledge their parents will return again at the end of the work day. Therefore, children with a secure attachment style will turn to their caregiver or support person for comfort when they experience anxiety. This gave them the confidence to stand independently, and they have learned effective coping mechanisms to deal with challenges in life as they trust themselves (and others). This is the kind of behavior that is associated with a secure attachment style, and it is the most healthy of attachment styles to develop.

In adult life, someone with this style of attachment will be comfortable with and trust other people, as well as trust themselves. They will be comfortable with being close to others, while being confident enough to stand on their own too. Adults with a secure attachment style will be dependable, and they will often depend on others, delegating tasks, and trusting these will be done. They will also have learned successful methods of dealing with their stressors and coping with pressure in a healthy way. These adults display confidence and are secure in their own abilities, yet they know when and how to get social support. This makes them socially well adjusted.

According to Cherry (2020), mothers have a significant influence on the formation of the secure attachment style in their infants by being responsive and meeting their child's needs. In adult relationships, it is also quite easy to see why a person with a secure attachment style will be a more responsive and responsible partner. Cherry also refers to the Hazan and Shaver study where 56% of participants rated themselves as exhibiting a secure attachment style. Therefore, most people who were raised in stable childhood homes will tend to develop a secure attachment style.

To improve or develop your secure attachment style, you can develop skills like communication, empathy, compassion, understanding, assertiveness, and acceptance. These can be acquired through activities such as counseling, group discussions, reading to expand your knowledge, pursuing activities that build your self-esteem such as art and going to the gym, and also doing family tasks together such as cleaning, cooking, and engaging in hobbies. This is how you will learn to respect others, develop your sense of self, become empowered, learn to listen to other points of view, and build a sense of belonging. By becoming more caring, you can also reinforce your partnership as you engage in selfless activities such as making your partner breakfast, helping them with projects, and comforting them when they are in distress.

- **Anxious Attachment Style**

We all remember growing up with a child in our class who was shifty as they were suspicious and evasive. They didn't rush up to greet their parents, yet they wanted to be with caregivers at the start and end of the day. Children with this attachment style tend to be moody and depressive. They seem to wait for disaster to strike. To try and fit in, people with anxious attachment style tend to be people-pleasers.

A child with this style of attachment will tend towards being anxious about changes such as being dropped off at school. They will struggle to adjust to new situations or display feelings of abandonment quickly. They tend to be clingy and will gravitate towards power figures such as teachers or bullies who they will follow. Children who display self-doubt and an inability to work independently will likely fall in this attachment grouping. By avoiding situations or people who push them towards being independent, they will become easily manipulated by others. Peer opinion of them is what matters most to them. Needless to say, people pleasing can become a serious concern with this attachment style.

As adults, people with anxious attachment style struggle to stand out as leaders, and they will rather assume a follower role. They easily develop a mob mentality, doing as they are told. Secretly, they don't trust others, which is why they will often pick fights or pick on those with a shy nature to meet the approval of their peers. By running others down, they may make themselves feel better. Anxiety is always prevalent in their lives, though they probably deny this. Their insecurities may manifest as temper tantrums and refusing to participate in family activities, and they often withdraw since they don't know how to really process joy as they often live in fear.

Adults with anxious attachment styles have probably grown up in homes where their mother and other caregiver was not available to comfort or assure them. They have developed a reluctance to connect to others and feel like they are not worthy enough to be successful or to be loved by someone else. Fear of rejection and abandonment often manifest in their relationships. This can be displayed as aggression and rejection behavior (Cherry, 2020).

This attachment style is relatively rare, and according to the study mentioned earlier, only 19% of adults find this style as being characteristic of their coping skills. While this style may be less prevalent, we often find adults who display aspects of it in certain situations in their lives based on their own experiences and mental constructs.

You need to display great empathy when communicating with and connecting to someone with anxious attachment style. Building secure connections that are reliable, while gently building boundaries, which all parties involved can respect, will be central to creating a lasting and more secure relationship.

Try to foster open communication, remembering that their thinking will quickly turn your words into confirmations that they are not good enough or threats that you will leave them. Saying something like "Don't you remember, I told you I would be late" can be interpreted as meaning "I am tired of your neediness, and you are a burden." Instead, using careful phrasing such as "I am sorry for being late and causing you to worry. Something outside of my control happened" will be better interpreted as you have removed their cause for anxiety and self-blame. Your communication should soothe their worries and anxieties. It is possible to help your anxiety-driven partner to accept themselves and accept you. This will foster trust, which is something they sorely lack and will diffuse their anxieties.

- **Avoidant Attachment Style**

Starting with parental neglect and emotional unavailability, this style of attachment causes children to treat both their parents and strangers with equal disinterest. While children who form this attachment style become independent adults, they are not connected to their social circles or families. They are not confident, and they merely continue onwards on their own steam with little to no regard for those around them.

Children with this style of attachment tend to be loners, and since they don't trust the world at all, they will easily hide away, struggling to make friends or relate to others. Often, some childhood trauma may trigger this style of attachment (or lack of attachment), and they will struggle to play with others. Praise will always be met with suspicion, and they will not take punishment well either. To them, being corrected is a negative criticism, which confirms their suspicions about the world. These children will struggle to be close to anyone, even their own family, and they will avoid getting involved in anything. Therefore, they tend towards an anxious personality type too. Life is stressful to them since they don't believe the world can be trusted or that they can ever simply relax.

Adults with this attachment style tend towards being loners too. They often become suspicious of their partners if they are in a relationship, and paranoia is often a part of their personality. They will struggle to fit in at work, and they often have very few friends. In their professional careers, they will probably have held several jobs as they may struggle to progress within an organization since they will suspect the structures, their peers, and their bosses. Self-preservation might make them quit their jobs unnecessarily as they anticipate being fired or a company going under without valid reason. We might even find the divorce rate being quite high among people with this attachment style as it is incredibly difficult to remain in a relationship with someone who is constantly busy self-preserving, and they don't trust their partner at all.

To recover from dismissive-avoidant attachment style, you need to cultivate an awareness of others and improve your self-awareness. Charity work can help you develop compassion and empathy. While avoidant behavior may, on the surface, make you feel safe, it is damaging to your personal development and indicates a low self-esteem. In your relationships, being avoidant or dismissive diminishes enjoyment and can even affect your sex life negatively. Everything in your relationship can seem to have a negative connotation when you struggle with forming lasting attachments.

When recovering from dismissive-avoidant attachment style, you should focus on self-acceptance, discovering how you can relate to others, perhaps attend communication classes, and practice healthy expression of your emotions. As a child, your curiosity and interest in the world was suppressed, and you need to excavate this through a process of finding your inner child again. Find out what you want, discover your needs, and find meaningful and safe ways to fulfill these. Whichever interventions you choose, you will need to keep your safety and stress relief in mind. Bungee jumping off a bridge may seem like a drastic solution to finding an emotion; however, the resulting emotion (fear) will not help you connect to others or cultivate compassion.

Sadly, 25% of the Hazan and Shaver study reported themselves as displaying dismissive-avoidant attachment style when it came to their relationships. This does not bode well for the intimate relationships which these individuals engage in.

- **Anxious-Avoidant Attachment Style**

Someone with disorganized or fearful-avoidant attachment behavior will show a mix of avoidant and resistant behavior—they become ambivalent to their lives, events, and people close to them. Children with this style of attachment will be clingy to their caregivers one moment and then avoid them the next. Adults will display traits from the secure attachment style, anxious attachment style, and dismissive-avoidant attachment style, often seeming like a chameleon that can't make up its mind about people or relationships.

With this attachment style, children develop apprehension about their world. They almost expect bad things to happen. This can stop them from living with joy as they tend to become pessimistic. They will struggle to communicate or articulate themselves clearly, and they will seem to be disinterested in everything since they are really just incredibly unsure about the world and the people in it. Children with this attachment style will struggle to form close relationships and friendships, and they often struggle to relate to others. Feeling all alone, they will suffer from anxiety and will not have effective coping mechanisms in place.

As adults, people who have this attachment style will struggle with their relationships. They will not know how to make real connections to their partners, often simply being in a relationship since it is the socially acceptable thing to do, not because they really love or care for the other person. This is not something they intentionally do or feel either. Instead, it is just an inability on their part to connect and this often needs to be redressed. With no solid connections or support, people with this attachment (or avoidance) style tend to be anxious about life. Clearly, they feel all alone, which is a scary way to go through life.

Their past will be littered with instances of parents who were addicts or emotionally unwell. As children, people with this style of attachment probably suffered repeated neglect and illnesses that went untreated. Abuse was a constant presence, but this was hidden by caregivers who, by turns, seemed to act in their child's best interest one minute while neglecting them the next. This created a childhood that confused the child and led them to habitually mimick these conflicting behaviors. Adults with this behavior style struggle to make decisions, and they become inconsistent and can't be depended on to uphold their end in a relationship.

While it is unclear what percentage of the population falls within this style of behavior, it is important to be mindful that people with this style will act with inconsistency, and you may feel confused by them. To help your partner who displays this style, you need to be meticulous in your consistency. Help them build routines, celebrate successes, and be ready to constantly assure them that they are doing okay. Be careful not to create doubts in them.

Attachment Styles and Relationships

Image 3: mohamed_hassan on pixabay. How you form attachments will also play a significant role in your relationships whether these are platonic, romantic, or familial. Your attachment will determine how you resolve conflict, how you relate to others, and how you use or respect boundaries.

- **Secure Attachment**

John has been happily married for 20 years. He adores his wife, but he also respects that she is a working woman and will be away from home at times. He is concerned about her when she travels, but he knows she is a good driver and will call him to let him know she is safe when she arrives at her destination. While they have been married for 20 years, the couple still enjoy a healthy sex life, and they are not strangers to intimacy. John can quickly see when something is bothering his wife. Though he always asks her what is wrong and can he help, he also knows she wants to be in charge of her life and will deal with things in her own way. While many of John's colleagues have expressed concern with John's wife being away on business often, he chooses not to become jealous as he knows they share a good relationship with open communication. As a whole, John is optimistic about his relationship, and he is happy to see his wife at the end of the day.

The above example illustrates how someone who has a secure attachment style responds in a relationship. People with this style of behavior and decision making are able to respect the boundaries of their partners, and they feel comfortable creating and maintaining their own relationship boundaries. This creates a healthy structure in the relationship. Securely attached adults will be confident enough in themselves and in their partners, and there is no need for jealousy, clingy, or needy behavior. Despite this, they are not afraid of expressing their intimate needs and affections, and they eagerly support their partners in appropriate ways. These individuals are confident and optimistic in their own abilities and their role within the relationship. They often experience a deep and spiritual connection to their partner, without the pressure of being needy or dependent.

- **Anxious Attachment**

Sara is not content in her relationship. She is convinced her partner is cheating on her, and she suffers from chronic anxiety attacks when she thinks about their relationship as she fears being single. Despite her partner constantly telling her everything is okay between them, she still does not believe him, and she is mentally trying to prepare herself for their eventual break-up. When she finds a lipstick mark on his shirt one day after work, she goes ballistic, packs her bags, and prepares to storm out of their apartment. When her partner tries to explain, she simply cries hysterically.

People like Sara are what could be termed a hot mess. They are clingy, needy, and they constantly want to be told that everything is okay by their partners. Everything in their behavioral repertoire centers around getting outside approval. Everything that happens within the relationship is a drama, and they do not handle changes easily. They seem to be ready to run at the drop of a hat, and though they desire the security of a relationship, they are quick to ruin it by being anxious and emotional. Being demanding, they create relationship stress, and they tend to be jealous and suspicious of their partners. With so many negative emotions stirring in people with anxious attachment styles, it is no surprise that they tend to be pessimistic about their relationships, seeing everything in a negative light.

- **Avoidant Attachment**

James has built a reputation as a cold-hearted man. Though he has had many relationships, he has yet to display anything by way of affection or love to his partners. Secretly, he has had multiple relationships while already with a particular partner, and having a one-night relationship seems to be of little concern to him. When his partner finds out and challenges him, he is quick to end the relationship. This does not seem to bother him at all, and he quickly launches into a new relationship.

He is a social butterfly, and while he engages in many relationships, these rarely become intimate. When he starts to develop feelings for his partner or they ask him questions, he tends to leave the relationship without any warning or he starts to act sullen.

The avoidant-attachment style can be extremely hard on couples and in relationships. Like the above example, someone with avoidant-attachment style tends to be emotionally distant, seeming to be cold and aloof. Becoming emotionally invested is not likely to happen with someone who does not show any affection. People like James seem incapable of really feeling anything, and they often lack the commitment to remain faithful to their relationships. They are not confident enough to build a lasting connection and commitment scares them. This is why they will often bounce from one failed relationship right into the next relationship without seeming to care at all.

Secretly, they are afraid of commitment and getting hurt. This is why they may seem frivolous, and they will sometimes cause their relationships to fail intentionally to avoid commitment. When a relationship ends, they experience fear, and this can cause them to act out in a passive-aggressive way, becoming sulky and vindictive. Despite not being able to be in a meaningful relationship, people with avoidant-attachment disorder also struggle to be on their own.

- **Anxious-Avoidant Attachment**

Lisa has always wanted to be married for as long as she could remember. Sadly, she often ends up in broken relationships where she is abused by her partners. Relationships with her are characterized by trauma and conflict. While Lisa desires commitment, she both chases and pushes away her partners. As a result, she has become bitter and reluctant to communicate and open up. Lisa's biggest fear is losing out on love, and she will launch into a relationship with an almost desperate passion.

When her partners push her towards things she is not comfortable with, she quickly gives in and does as they want. Even when she feels uncomfortable with what someone does to her, she does not say anything, being too anxious they will not like her for it.

The anxious-avoidant attachment style is a combination of being afraid of a relationship, wanting it since being alone seems even more terrifying, yet wanting to avoid contact. It is a most confusing way to enter and sustain a relationship. Therefore, people with this attachment style often find themselves in chaotic or tumultuous relationships marked by conflict, obsession, and neglect.

While people with this attachment style crave the security and comfort of a relationship, they also push their loved ones away, before reeling them in with drama again when faced with the possibility of being alone. Despite wanting love, these people are afraid of being alone, and they keep themselves from committing and becoming deeply involved in a relationship.

Relationships with this attachment style in one or more of the partners is characterized by pessimism, and they lack effective or constructive boundaries. This causes resentment between the partners, and with a lack of communication, drama follows. Obsessive behavior and jealousy, as well as avoidance, are also very common in these relationships.

Each of these attachment styles originate from a specific series of circumstances, and they manifest in different ways during the stages of life. Powerful forces are at play during our life stages, and only in understanding these and how they impact on our continued attachment styles can we begin to lead our best lives.

Chapter 2:

An Overview of

Attachment Through

Different Life Stages

Image 4: maz-Alph from Pixabay. Life is marked by many stages, ranging from infancy and childhood to later life. During these stages, we change, adapt, or stagnate. This is all dependent on our behavior styles and our ability to engage in self-reflection

and willingness to improve. By looking at the various development stages, we can also gain insight into how attachment styles form and how these influence us throughout our lives.

Attachment in Infancy and Childhood

During the early formative years, from being born to 18 months old, babies develop their attachment through crying and clinging to their primary caregivers. Most of these behaviors are instinctive and are motivated by a biological need such as hunger or comfort. When the primary caregiver leaves the young infant, they become anxious and cry (Ackerman, 2020a). As children grow older, they start to form their own internal thinking paradigm, and based on the reliability of their caregivers, they form beliefs about the reliability of their world and of themselves.

When the child receives a balanced support and mirroring system from their caregivers, they develop a settled brain chemistry, affecting the hormones and neurotransmitters in the brain. Reese (2007) supports this in finding that the levels of stress-management by cortisol production is set during infancy in relation to experiences. This, in turn, affects the emotional spectrum and control that children develop and carry through into adolescence and adulthood. The emotional range will also influence the attachment styles that develop with anxious-avoidant attachment on one end, secure attachment in the middle, and anxious-resistant attachment at the other end.

Research into childhood attachment styles have delivered much information, but for the layman's application, it is useful to know what to look for in identifying your child's particular attachment style, and sadly, this is something many new parents are completely unprepared for.

- **Secure Attachment**

In children, seeing behavior like being helpful, respectful, trusting, and resilient, as well as class-room participation and the willingness to participate in more novel or complex tasks, all indicate a secure attachment style has developed. Children with this attachment style tend towards developing empathy and the ability to put themselves in someone else's shoes, to see things through someone else's eyes. This leads to the cultivation of trust and reliability.

Parents tend to be responsible and present when their children form this attachment style. If their child cries, they are quick to soothe their anxiety, and this develops the child's ability to trust and interact with people. They engage in healthy play and bonding with their parents and caregivers. When the parent leaves the home, they ensure their child is in the care of a reliable substitute caregiver to ensure that anxiety is minimal, and they return soon, thereby assuring their child that they can be counted on.

- **Anxious-Avoidant Attachment**

With children, this style results in behavior such as struggling in stressful situations, being withdrawn and anxious, not forming friendships or relationships with their caregivers, and the display of negative emotions such as anger, bullying, deceitfulness, and an inability to relate to the emotions of others. These children struggle with expressing themselves, and they quickly pick on others to make themselves feel better. Being with others causes them stress and anxiety, and therefore, they distance themselves more, preferring to be loners.

Children with this behavior style tend to come from homes where the environment is volatile and there is no stability between them and their caregivers. They may be left alone for long periods of time or they may not be soothed when they suffer anxiety. As a result, they do not trust new situations or strangers. Due to these children having such anger in them, they display aggressive behavior towards those they interact with. Mothers are often not available, which is a key factor towards children developing the anxious-avoidant attachment style.

- **Anxious-Resistant Attachment**

Found on the opposite end of the behavior range, children with this style of behavior tend to be excessively needy and clingy. They want to constantly be with their primary caregivers, and they follow after them like puppies. If they are separated from their parents or caregivers, they tend to have an overly emotional reaction such as crying, screaming, or becoming agitated, yet when the caregiver returns, they often avoid them. They struggle to relate to their own age group and prefer to stick to their caregiver or rather be alone. This leads to isolation.

Families of children who display anxious-resistant attachment are often abusive or neglect these children for large parts of the day. This quickly teaches the child they can only count on themselves. Therefore, when they are placed in a situation of needing to depend on or show affection to an adult, they react with uncertainty and even aggression. Early childhood for these children may include physical, emotional, and sexual abuse, which later manifests in deviant behavior and social awkwardness. They may also have been bullied by a caregiver who teased them when they were in distress.

- **Disorganized Attachment**

Children with this attachment style are like confused chameleons. They have no solid strategy for coping in life, and they fall from one type of behavior to the other. Behavior can include becoming aggressive, disruptive, emotional, and isolating themselves. Instead of looking to other people for support, they see people as a threat and respond negatively to them.

The childhood home of children with this attachment style is often a place of confusion. They may be raised by a single parent who has a range of new partners entering and leaving the home. Or, they may suffer with one or both parents being abusive or given to addictions, which cause the parents to act inconsistently. At a very young age, these children both want and avoid attention. They will ask for hugs and then run away. When activities are being performed, they seem confused about participating. A few years later, they will begin taking on the parental role, doing chores that are beyond their years and often parenting their parent if that person is given a reduced mental capacity at times due to addiction.

Attachment Styles: Factors That Influence Your Kids

The attachment style of parents can also have a significant impact on the behavioral style that children develop. It is not a guarantee that a parent who has a secure attachment style will necessarily raise a child who has the same attachment style, though the likelihood of this increases. Likewise, when a parent is themselves given to an anxious-resistant behavior style (or any other unhealthy behavior style), they will have a larger likelihood of raising a child who suffers from an unhealthy attachment style.

Attachment styles also do not happen as a result of one experience, nor do they magically (or genetically) manifest. Rather, it is a gradual process where a multitude of experiences or massively traumatic singular events have a negative impact on a child's development. Abuse is a sure indicator of the possible development of unhealthy behavior styles. These issues children develop and try to process by creating an unhealthy behavior style are not something children will outgrow. It will not improve on its own, and your child will carry it with them into adulthood if you do not take action to intercede and intervene at an early age.

Interventions and counseling need to be directed at an appropriate age group, and it should be remembered that a child is not a mini-adult. Therefore, you can't talk your child out of their unhealthy development style, nor can you beat them out of it (which is what many parents try to do). Rather, you need to focus on the preoperational stage of development that young children experience, which mostly deals with the senses, particularly sight.

Using activities such as playing games, drawing, making art, and singing songs are a great way to communicate with young children. This will help challenge their unhealthy behavior styles and thinking without raising conflict or causing anxiety. In activities such as building puzzles, playing, making and creating art, and performing, young children can be helped to improve their attachment to people and friends. Over time, and through careful and consistent interventions, children can move from the more volatile end of the behavior range towards the healthier secure attachment style of behavior.

Try these activities suggested by West-Olatunji (2019) to heal the wounds caused by harmful or unhealthy attachment styles and facilitate healthy bonding:

- **Popsicle People**

Using popsicle sticks, glitter, wool, and other craft items, create a stick figure for each member in the family with your child. Let your child use this opportunity to wrap up the figures as they feel fit, allowing them to express their feelings and begin to communicate to their caregivers with the dolls acting as intermediaries. By showing your child you can take care of their doll, they will begin to see that you can take care of them, fostering trust and confidence.

- **Feeling Faces**

This is another popular bonding and counseling technique that can be easily used. Printing out several children's faces on A4 pages, you encourage your child to touch and talk to the faces, identifying the emotions, and reacting to the emotions. This is a great way to help your child learn compassion and identify with other people's feelings, which is so vital for making connections to others. For really young children, you can encourage them to trace the emotions on the lips and eyes of the pictures. Then you can help your child to mimic these expressions. As an added bonus, it can help repair your relationship with your child since we instantly feel close to someone we learn positive things from.

- **Storytelling**

While young children lack the vocabulary or ability to tell stories, they need to be given a chance to express themselves. The important thing here is to let them tell the story their way; you should not interrupt them or correct them. Asking questions is fine, but accept what they choose to say, and how they make up the story. The child can use drawings, cartoons, or pictures to tell their story.

Freehand drawings are often used for this. If your child is resistant to communicating or expressing interest in narrating a story, you could try reading a picture book to them and asking them in a gentle and non-threatening way about the pictures. This would draw them into communications and develop a healthy exchange and encourage bonding.

- **Puppets or a Doll's House**

This is an expansion of the above storytelling idea, but here you use puppets, toys, and other tangible objects to tell stories. You can begin to teach moral values and the importance of having people in your life whom you can depend on to your child. Be careful to keep your stories and words age appropriate.

- **Play Dough**

Expression is a healthy way for children to deal with their emotions, and using material such as play dough gives a fun dimension to this exercise. The goal is to draw the child out of their shell and help them externalize their internal conflict. This is how you will help the young child deal with their inner traumas and find healthy expression and connection. The nice thing about play dough is that it encourages tactile interaction, and children naturally love to touch it, which may help you break through some emotional barriers that trauma has created in your child.

Attachment in Adolescence and Young Adulthood

While attachment styles follow the same patterns as established in early childhood, there are a few changes that sneak in during adolescence and young adulthood. For starters, this is when people start to become more aware of and involved in relationships. These relationships are not only physical need based, such as a baby needing to be fed or comforted. It also includes romantic relationships, and since teenagers and young adults are still trying to find out who they are in relation to others, this is a particularly vulnerable stage of development. Attachment styles may change, worsening or improving depending on the relationship experiences and successes that the teen and young adult enjoys.

While attachment styles can be loosely understood as a working model for behavior that we all develop, this becomes infinitely more complicated during adolescence. While a child who has developed a secure attachment base during early childhood is certainly more prepared to face adolescence, they can still become unsettled when they face a situation or experience in their teens they are not prepared for. Once poor self-esteem develops, this may signal the beginning of a web of negative experiences and harmful decisions and behavior.

Since children instinctively model the behavior they see in their parents, they will usually copy their parents' behavior patterns. This could possibly be a worst case of the sins of the father (or mother) being revisited on their children. With parents who are unstable in their behavior styles, the children will inevitably suffer similar behavioral decisions unless intervention is implemented or a stronger role-model affects the child's decision-making formation.

Choosing to intervene and help teenagers form better behavior styles is about breaking the vicious cycle and preventing early adult psychological deviant behavior and ill-health as a result of conditions such as depression, mania, obsessive compulsive behaviors, and even more serious conditions that are linked to early mortality. When considering an intervention, you would have to look at the displayed behavior of the teen and evaluate whether this indicates neediness, avoidance, attention seeking, how the teen calms themselves, and how they handle anxiety or stress. This will provide some indication of whether the adolescent has moved from their stable (or even their unhealthy) childhood behavior style and whether they are coping with the demands and stressors of adolescent life.

Teenagers or adolescents with unhealthy behavior styles will struggle with understanding emotions, relationships, and they will not successfully relate to others. This could give rise to serious conditions such as attention deficit hyperactivity disorder (ADHD), obsessive-compulsive disorder (OCD), and other negative labels being applied to them by their peers and authority figures such as teachers.

When an adolescent or even a young adult is exposed to multiple traumas or challenges that they have a negative reaction to, this is known as cumulative developmental trauma (CDT), and it is responsible for many teens and young adults experiencing a disintegration and dissociation from their previously successful behavior styles. This can often result in post-traumatic stress disorder (PTSD), which will further develop unhealthy behavior styles that are anxiety and avoidance based instead of the individual searching for a positive or secure solution. In practice, we often see this with teenagers who engage in risky sexual behavior or suffer a romantic break-up that results in depression, tension, agitation, anxiety, and in the end, avoidance of relationships in general.

What makes the adolescent and young adult stage of development so traumatic and potentially crucial to the individual's healthy development of an effective attachment style is that this is a stage where there are massive external factors influencing their development. A teenager will face peer pressure, bullying, sexual pressure, and hormonal pressures as they try to find who and what they are. Likewise, a young adult is at the cusp of being a "child" and becoming a "successful adult." This means they will face new challenges such as tertiary studies, evolving relationships, possible parentage, entering the employment market where bullying can again surface, and the heart-rending question of "what to do you want to be" applying pressures on them.

Attachment traumas at these crucial stages will have a significant impact on the resulting behavior styles. Getting help and support during these life stages is vital to developing or maintaining a secure attachment style. For teenagers, dealing with relationships on a romantic level is often incredibly traumatic. They have moved from the cute puppy-love stage to burgeoning intimacies, and often this is accompanied by raging emotions such as love, closeness, dependence, betrayal, anger, and jealousy. These can lead to serious harm being done to the previous behavior style they had formed. While parents may want to step in and shield their teenagers from the "bad world," this is something the adolescent child or young adult needs to deal with and learn from. So, how does a parent support their adolescent child or their young adult child who is possibly heading out on their own for the first time?

For adolescents, given that they are in new situations and may lack the skills to cope, it is instrumental to combine support with helping them develop coping skills. These techniques can be useful to help foster and protect a more secure attachment style (Reachout.com, n.d.):

- **Encourage Communication**

While you can often see that your child is in pain, you may often feel stuck on the outside talking at the walls they have put up. Fostering and encouraging communication from a young age will help to open avenues for support. In your communications, be careful to realize that this is not about you preaching to them on how to do things (like you did things), but it is rather about giving your adolescent or young adult child a way to vent, release, process, and evaluate their feelings and their possible actions in a healthy way. They talk, and you listen. When you do talk, be careful to talk *with* them and *not at* them. In the infancy interventions, you learned to listen as your child told the story, and this should not change when they become teenagers. Only if they ask, should you offer solutions. You can't live their lives, so don't.

- **Step Away**

When you are young, every issue seems like Mt. Everest, so help your adolescent step away and find a balance between being with people and being on their own. They need to realize that the issue they are dealing with is not their whole life. As the saying goes: it's not a bad life, just a bad day. Developing life perspective is a vital life skill and will help to remove a lot of the anxiety that creates unhealthy behavior styles.

- **Develop Passion Paths**

Finding joy is a great way to build confidence and develop a secure attachment style. Therefore, encourage your adolescent child or young adult to engage in their favorite hobby (which isn't hanging out with friends) or doing a self-building activity such as art or reading.

With effective repetition and application of the idea of making a safe place or pattern of doing to which the child can return, it will become a habitual behavior that will build self-esteem and release anxieties.

- **Healthy Habits**

A healthy body houses a healthy mind. Encourage and model healthy behavior such as healthy eating, not binging, exercising, and practicing self-care. These routines also help form healthy attachment behavior styles.

- **Stress Solutions**

We can only use the solutions we are familiar with. So, teaching your child from a young time to practice healthy interventions such as breathing techniques, yoga, tai chi, or meditation can be a great way to help them deal with the tensions of discovering relationships and love. It will also help them stay healthy, reduce anxiety, and build self-esteem as they realize they can control their bodies and engage in self-care, which feels good too.

- **Positive Self-Talk**

Doubt is the result of anxiety, and this often results in anxiety and fear-driven behavior such as negative self-talk. Ensuring that your adolescent or young adult is aware of their inner thoughts and knows they can control what they think is a highly effective way to create healthy behavior management patterns. Using positive affirmations can counter negative external influences such as bullying, peer pressure, and relationship confusion.

- **Creating Healthy Examples**

Children who have secure and balanced parents or caregivers are more prone to be positive, secure, and independent (self-assured). Hence, you should model what you are seeking to create in your child. This does not mean you need to be perfect. Instead, this means you need to show them how you deal with issues and what behavior you use to live a successful and balanced life. Clearly, knocking back several quarts a night after a stressful day is not the example they need. However, seeing you spend some time listening to music and then writing in a journal or dancing while you make supper will help them approach life with confidence and self-empowerment.

Mid-Life Attachment

Mid-life can be an equally trying period of development in life. This is when our values can be challenged by factors such as relationship satisfaction, job satisfaction, introspection, and the involvement and evolution of our growing families, and the supposed mid-life crisis. These all contribute to building tension and anxiety, and in sexual terms, this is often when sexual dysfunction often appears.

In mid-life, relationships also face their most challenging times as parents start to age and also have to deal with their adolescent children's life crisis. The dynamics between relationship partners (including the partnership between children and parents) change, and this can cause serious mental strain and divorce rates often increase in the age group of the 50s and 60s. This can be partially attributed to mid-life strain (Whitbourne, 2013). The reality is that people often drift apart in this life-stage as they struggle to deal with crisis and stressors. Long-term relationships can come undone as partners lose focus on each other, and they often become bored and disillusioned with the life they have created for themselves.

A good example of this is the Oscar winning movie, *American Beauty* (1999). This movie shows several factors that challenge and dissolve the primary relationship, including conflict with the children, partners losing touch, personal inadequacy, and low self-esteem, which all contribute to chaos and interpersonal conflict. Though your life may not be quite as dramatic, there could be similarities in your relationship challenges and how this affects your behavior style. Where you may have been happily married and secure in your attachments, you could find yourself suffering anxiety and dissociation or avoidance, which might lead to the ending of your relationships. So, how can you ensure the success and security of your relationships and attachment style?

- **Positive Partners**

Be mindful to focus on the positive assets of your partner. If you dwell on your partner's flaws, you will not want to spend time with them. However, if you pay more attention to their positive points, you will be more likely to want to be with them and see less of their flaws. This reduces relationship conflicts. People argue about their (or their partner's) flaws, never about their plus points, so focus on those.

- **Think Yourself Together**

The saying "out of mind, out of heart" is a sad reality. When you are thinking of your partner in a positive way, you will not be tempted to stray outside of the relationship. You will also feel more content and be less inclined to question your "success" (which is often more in your mind than a reality). Complement this with phoning your partner to express concern or interest in them. You used to do this when you were younger, only then, it was flirting with your partner, why can't you do so now?

- **Avoid Multitasking**

While we may be pressured by busy lives to multi-task, this takes your focus away from your partner and your relationship. Focus on spending time together that is yours alone. This doesn't have to be a holiday or some novel gesture. Instead, focus on making it a routine (which positively builds your coping skills and behavior style) such as a Saturday bed brunch. No one wants to feel like they have someone's divided time, so focus on your partner and on yourself, not on outside distractions.

- **Use Challenges as Glue**

In mid-life, we often feel like we haven't accomplished all that we wanted. We become more and more aware of time running out and our fast-approaching mortality. However, we will probably live longer than we think, and there is always time to expand our sense of self and do things to make us feel alive again. The important thing is to use challenges and adventures such as going on a road trip or bungee jumping as activities that keep you together with your partner. Just because you have been together for 20 years does not mean your relationship is fixed or should stagnate. Be assertive and communicate about the life challenges you still wanted to embrace.

- **Bond With Time**

Relationships take time. If you are only spending a few hours a week together due to work, activities with the kids, relaxing with your friends, then you are gearing up your relationship for dissociation and are engaging in avoidance. Spend time together as you continue to strengthen ties, reinforce each other's sense of worth, and deepen your love and affection.

- **Turn on Affection and Love**

Flowing from the above intervention, you should continue to share affection and expand on your intimacies within the relationship. While sex is said to stagnate in mid-life and die completely by later life, this does not have to be the case. Be open and communicative about your needs. There is nothing wrong with flirty behavior to please and pleasure your partner as long as this is well communicated and reciprocated. Intimacy is a powerful binding force. It makes both partners feel a boost to their self-esteem to feel needed and wanted by their partner.

Attachment in Later Life

Later life can be a more traumatic experience than many people realize or prepare themselves for. Challenges such as reaching pensionable age, having to adjust to life at home (and not at work), rediscovering your partner, or dealing with the loss of a partner can create massive anxiety and, with a slow decline of mental functioning, this can really challenge your coping skills and behavior style. The people in your life may also have changed significantly from who they were when you started out together, and if you have neglected your relationship, this may bring disparity and discontent. The major stressor is the possibility of losing your partner and becoming single again. In addition to this, we have to deal with the reality that we will face our own death.

Behavior patterns can become problematic at this age as this is often when people stop growing and lack the ability to adjust and cope with their life experiences. Often, people believe the elderly are set in their ways, which can create trauma in the relationship to their significant others, their adult children, and grandchildren.

Some common issues that face late-life adults include:

Depressive Disorders

With failing health and physical decline, the sense of self will begin to decline, and elderly people often begin to suffer from depressive episodes. Combined with the loss of a partner or the financial strain of being a pensioner, this can easily result in serious depression disorders. This, in turn, negatively impacts on health, which worsens the pensioner's emotional state. Late life suicide is becoming much more prevalent than before.

Anxiety Disorders

Due to depression, failing health, and the decline of the chemicals that the brain requires to maintain an emotional balance, anxiety disorders are also prone to increase in late life. Maintaining a healthy life outlook, keeping the brain alert with activities, and engaging with your world will greatly help to boost a sense of purpose and help negate anxiety.

Bipolar Disorders

While this disorder mostly sets in during your early twenties, it can also appear in late life. Perhaps this is due to anxiety, chemical imbalances, and declining health; however, the effects are equally devastating. The dizzying highs and dismal lows associated with bipolar disorders can manifest in late life, with the additional burden of age-related medication such as blood pressure, heart, kidney, and lung medications complicating the chemical processes of the body.

It can place a strain on your relationships, and when combined with other disorders (which it often does), you may begin to lose the ability to function in the stressful situation that comes with daily independent life.

Oppositional Defiant Disorder

This disorder often manifests in the elderly. They may be defiant, engage in rage filled outbursts, lament how no one comes to see them (yet they don't go see anyone themselves), and they might even become spiteful or vengeful (such as disinheriting their "ungrateful" children). This can completely destroy your existing behavior style as you become given over to anxiety and even paranoia. Antisocial behavior will soon follow, and many elderly people become recluse, not wanting to venture out into the world where their tempers are easily triggered.

Age-Related Disorders

Other age-related disorders such as dementia, Alzheimer's disease, and Parkinson's disease can also severely challenge your coping ability, behavior, and decision-making paradigms. This may require careful management and even late life care at a professional facility.

While these disorders can be intimidating, and it may seem to indicate that growing old will be an unpleasant experience, this is not so. By being proactive and informed, you can ensure you remain vital, behaviorally adapted, and maintain close connections to the people you love. Here are some suggestions for maintaining and creating a secure late-life behavior style:

- **Rebuild Your Body**

While many elderly people have simply accepted their physical decline, this need not be the norm. When you look good, you feel good, and this can have amazing effects on both your psyche and mind. Taking care of yourself physically by doing some activity to promote flexibility and mobility can have a significant effect on your self-esteem, independence, and keep your emotions more stable too. Take up a physical hobby such as tai chi, go for massages, spoil yourself with a good skin care routine, and take care of your teeth. Smile daily and allow yourself to have fun, using your mind to interact with other people instead of sinking into your frail body and feeling despair.

- **Adapt**

One of the worst things you can do in late life is to sit still and lose interest in the world around you. This may seem like a great way to minimize anxiety, since the world can become a really scary place to you in late life. Even more so with the recent worldwide shift in isolating behavior due to health concerns for the aged. However, you should engage in novel ideas, new inventions, and exciting changes that affect your world. If you can keep interested, you will be able to adapt to and remain interactive with the world and the people around you.

- **Medicate Appropriately**

Pills, different assistive aids, and other medical necessities are part of later life. However, by having an attitude towards your medical needs of simply clinging to life, you will not be doing yourself (or your behavior) any favors. By working with a skilled doctor, you will be able to plan your medical needs to not only keep you living but also help you stay alive and vital. You should supplement to keep your mind healthy and happy, and you should admit when you are feeling pressured or anxious and discuss treatment options with your doctor. Do not suffer in silence and withdraw. Connect and reach out, take charge of your emotions, and relate to others.

Chapter 3:

Getting Started With Some

Self-Awareness:

Emotionally Focused

Family Therapy

Techniques

Image 5: sweetlouise on pixaybay. While we often think focusing on our emotions means we should have a cry; this is not always what is behind it. Rather, it is the understanding and appropriate application of our emotions by identifying them in others and in ourselves. Through appropriate techniques, you can learn to respond in meaningful ways to the people you have relationships with and become responsible and aware of your own feelings and the impact of those feelings on your family.

What Is Emotionally Focused Family Therapy (EFFT)?

EFFT is a form of therapy that stems from the humanistic school of psychology, specifically from psychotherapeutic approaches to family relationships. It focuses on the family dynamic, how the individuals within the family interact with each other and themselves, and how this constructs their present experiences. During therapy sessions, attention is paid to the emotions of the family members as this indicates how they see and relate to the family experience. Emotions are the language of our behavior styles, and they inform us about our world, and they prompt action.

By interacting with and exploring the emotions within the family relationship, the therapist can help the family members discover and begin using new and more secure behavior patterns. EFFT is based on the work of psychologist John Bowlby who conducted research into and formulated much of attachment theory (Stavrianopoulos, 2019). The goal of EFFT is to foster increased emotional availability in parents and improved responsiveness in children. With the therapeutic interventions of EFFT, the role players in the family relationship are encouraged to be present and involved. This makes a huge difference in decreasing dissociation and avoidance within the relationship as the family experiences emotional involvement and growth.

When parents are emotionally available for their children, the children will feel assured and comforted. This will lead to more secure attachment behavior manifesting in the children, who will turn to their parents for support. When parents are emotionally unavailable, their children will resort to anxious and avoidant behavior. This creates points of contact between EFFT and attachment theory. According to Johnson (2009), the transactional nature of EFFT and attachment theory can be seen in a cause and effect interaction. The parent becomes more supportive, and the child becomes more open and trusting. When the self is developed, you will have more confidence and a more secure attachment style.

In essence, attachment theory and the development of a secure attachment behavior base thrive under the administration of EFFT. This can be summarized as follows:

- Attachment theory calls for a secure base of reference or safe home base to develop attachments from and EFFT creates this.
- While attachment theory helps us understand our deeper and more negative emotions such as pain, rejection, fear, and avoidance, EFFT helps to address these and build secure behavior.
- Emotions are the central guiding force and also the result of interactions and the resulting behaviors, and EFFT focuses on emotional development and healing.
- While behavior theories center around the person and their interaction with their world, EFFT focuses on the person's ability to change their world and their responses.

The feedback and effectiveness of EFFT is massively successful. The behavior styles of people, combined with emotional development and communication, create healthy narratives within the relationship. Its strong points include being supportive and respectful to clients, a history of 30+ years of empirical evidence, and continuing development in the field to address cultural differences and societal changes. The American Psychological Association (APA) has formally acknowledged EFFT as an effective treatment approach to treating depression, interpersonal conflict, past or suppressed trauma, and avoidant or anxious personality disorders (Church, 2017)

EFFT focuses on the emotions in a relationship (whether romantic or familial) that result from insecurities. Attachment-related insecurities can be addressed through facilitation of emotional development and skills building. Various techniques are used to assess emotional development and check whether the therapy participants are ready to progress to the next technique or level of therapy. It engages these techniques through several stages and steps that the family is guided through by the therapist who acts as a facilitator.

Stages and Steps of EFFT

In brief, there are three stages and nine steps to EFFT. The first four steps (stage one) are about reducing conflict and discovering which attachment styles the family (or relationship) members default to instinctively. Steps five through seven (stage two) is about creating more secure family relationships. In the remaining two steps (stage three), the therapist helps the family members discover more positive strategies and ways to interact. During these last steps, the family members also build their confidence in their ability to handle stressful events in a more proactive and positive way in the future. Therapy concludes when the family members can engage in new and positive ways in their daily life. This therapeutic process can be seen as follow:

- **Stage One: Cycle De-Escalation**

Step one: Identify conflict and issues in the relationship, such as a lack of communication and anxiety avoidance between the husband and wife.

Step two: Identify negative behavior and patterns that are linked to the conflict or issues, such as defensive shouting and neediness that happens when the partners threaten to part.

Step three: Evaluate attachment emotions that underpin the behavior of each partner in the relationship, such as anger masking fear of abandonment.

Step four: Rename the issues according to the emotions and attachment needs, such as seeing the partner's rage as being a declaration of insecurity, a need for belonging, and validation.

During this stage, the couple or family engage with the therapist, talking about the therapeutic setting, the therapist, their expectancies, and their past interactions. The end result of this stage is that the couple is no longer against each other, but rather against their past negative interactions. It is important that the couple is helped to identify the behavior patterns that fuel their attachment insecurities and begin to see this problem in a new way.

- **Stage Two: Changing Interaction Patterns**

Step five: Access and explore avoided emotions or emotions that are uncomfortable for the partners in the relationship such as fear, insecurities, and rage.

Step six: Foster acceptance of each partner's experience within the relationship.

Step seven: Achieve expression of each partner's experience and create new ways to bond within the relationship and nurture acceptance.

During this stage, the focus is on creating new experiences to replace the negative experiences and emotions that had previously existed in the relationship. Through an improved repertoire of communication skills, the partners are helped to better express their needs and feelings and show compassion with each other.

- **Stage Three: Consolidation and Integration**

Step eight: Begin a new relationship narrative to address the old problems. This is a process of actively and positively finding new solutions to the relationship (and behavior) problems.

Step nine: This is the conclusion where the couple take what they have learned and apply this to their problems within the home environment. While they are still unsure, they may cycle back to check in with the therapist and further consider step eight until they are able to effectively apply new solutions to old problems with confidence. This results in a secure attachment style.

Ways to Classify and Identify Attachment Styles

There are a plethora of different ways to classify attachment styles; some even call them love styles, but the reason to identify your style is to help you improve in your attachments and become more secure in your relationships. Taking a quick online test is one way to get an idea of which attachment style you tend to display. However, any test will only be as accurate as the honesty of your answers.

Now that you already know the basic tenets of the different attachment styles, you probably have some inclination of what style you tend towards. However, there are also a range of online quizzes and tests you can consider taking. Though they may not be definitive, they are a good place to start if you are still clueless as to your attachment style. Here are a few good tests to try:

- **Psychology Today**

This online test takes the form of answering a range of questions about your relationships and behavior by rating whether you agree with a statement or not. There are 50 statements, covering a diverse range of aspects of your behavior and relationships. Upon completion, you get a snapshot of your test results, with the option to purchase the full result. Complete the test at https://www.psychologytoday.com/za/tests/relationsh ips/relationship-attachment-style-test

- **Greatist.com**

If you want a bit more variety, you can try five different tests about attachment styles at this site where you follow the links to a range of tests. By trying different tests, you can get a broader view of your behavior and style of attachment. Find the tests at https://greatist.com/health/attachment-style-quizzes#1

- **Simple Questionnaire**

This short test, based on the test originally designed by Dr. Amir Levine and Rachel Heller, is a good place to start. Choose either 1—highly agree, 2—strongly disagree, or 3—neither to the statements below:

1. I do not enjoy it when my partner is close to me and asks questions.
2. Fears about my partner leaving me dominate my mind.
3. When my partner and I argue, I begin to doubt everything about us.

4. I avoid showing people how I feel as I believe they will not reciprocate, and I will be left feeling embarrassed.

5. When my partner is feeling depressed, I find it difficult to relate to them or offer comfort.

6. In my relationships, I feel no need to take action.

7. I worry that people will not like me once they get to know me.

8. Instead of being with my partner, I would rather be on my own.

9. When my partner is upset, I don't know how to help them find peace, so I retreat.

10. Being single is scary to me, and I would rather be in a relationship than on my own.

11. I loathe it when other people are dependent on me.

12. People think I am boring since I don't argue or fight in a relationship.

13. When my partner is away, I miss them, but once they are back, I wish they were gone.

14. My partner knows exactly what I want and need as I tell them clearly.

15. When my partner is standoffish, I believe I have somehow sinned or done something wrong.

16. Breakups are no problem for me. I get over them surprisingly quickly and move on to the next relationship.

17. If I break up from my partner, I fear being alone.
18. I know that when people are distant, it has nothing to do with me.

How did you score?

Scores of 30—36 (score of 2 in most questions) indicate you are predominantly secure attachment styled. You are in touch with your own emotions and those of the people around you. In your relationships, you care enough to participate since you have compassion, but you also realize it is not your responsibility to make others feel better. You invite discussions, and you respect other people's points of view.

If you scored a 1 in statements 1—5, 7, 9, 10, 12, 13, 15 and 17, you display characteristics of the anxious attachment style. You tend to struggle on your own, but when you are with people, you do not connect well and often blame yourself for this. Relationships do not comfort you, yet you hate being alone. Your partners may tend towards being abusive of you or they do not acknowledge how you feel since you don't express your feelings at all.

If you scored a 1 in statements 5, 6, 8, 11, 12, 16, you tend to be ambivalent in your relationships and have developed a fearful-avoidant attachment style that governs your behavior. You don't like being around people, but you also don't do well on your own.

With a score of 1 in statements 1, 5, 6, 8, 11, 16, this is characteristic of a dismissive-avoidant style of attachment. You struggle to form connections to other people, and you prefer your own company. Emotions are a mystery to you, and when people become emotional, you withdraw.

When looking at your past, you may begin to see instances where you have been directed towards the development of a certain attachment style. Abuse, neglect, failed relationships, dominating partners or bosses, and even sibling rivalry can lead to the development of an unhealthy attachment style. Events that made you fearful tend to create a fearful or anxious behavior style, and when you felt you had to crawl in your shell for protection in the past, you will likely still avoid real connection and intimacy.

Core Interventions and EFFT Exercises

There are a range of EFFT exercises that can be used in the therapeutic setting. Always, the goal is to achieve a specific end state based on the intervention technique or exercise.

- **Empathic Reflection**

Goal: The idea is for the therapist to hear their client out and develop an understanding of their client's needs and challenges.

Method: This is done by encouraging the client to talk about how they feel about the therapy process or even the therapist themselves. For example, when clients say things like, "I don't know what I am even doing here; I don't have a problem," this means they are engaging in avoidant and self-denial behavior.

- **Restructuring Interventions**

Goal: Here the therapist will interject new approaches or drive the discovery of new methods to deal with the problems that have been identified.

Method: This takes a discussion format where emotions are discussed in a transactional way. The therapist may lead the discussion or ask the client to do the theorizing, "If you feel like...and you try to...what would happen?"

- **Validation**

Goal: We all need to feel heard and valued. This is the goal of validation. It gives meaning to our pain, which can open the door to intervention.

Method: By acknowledging what a client says, and giving them the chance to really express emotions they may have denied even to themselves, it brings them out of the pit of despair and into a state of feeling supported.

- **Evocative Responding**

Goal: Sometimes, clients are unsure of how they actually feel about a past (or even current) trauma or behavior. The aim is to help them clarify this by probing their reactions and guiding them towards meaning.

Method: Direct questioning and careful summarizing of what the client says will help them to realize the underlying themes and unacknowledged emotions they are hiding.

- **Heightening**

Goal: When clients have hidden away their emotions, they may need to be pushed or directed to excavate these feelings through a heightening of related emotions.

Method: For instance, a therapist may stimulate the client's fear reaction or a feeling of sorrow by helping the client experience this through watching a video or seeing a picture.

- **Empathic Conjecture**

Goal: Helping clients to think critically about their emotions is a great way to help them interact with and consider the aspects of their feelings.

Method: By asking if the client sees themselves as being defensive, angry, avoidant, selfish, or needy, the therapist can help the client think about their own actions, behavior, and feelings.

- **Reframing**

Goal: Often used during the first stage of therapy, the therapist will rephrase what the client says to help reach a new understanding of the problem or to involve the client in the discussion.

Method: When the client says something like, "I feel so alone and no one understands me," the therapist may paraphrase this as, "Am I correct in saying that you feel disconnected and unvalued?"

- **Creating Enactments**

Goal: Creating a safe environment where the client can attempt different solutions to their problems.

Method: Through role-play, dialog, enactment, and even role reversals, the client can gain a better understanding of their problem and find healthy ways to address these, as well as seeing which approaches have the potential to work.

Finding an EFFT Therapist

When your secure attachment base is reasonably developed, you may be able to address minor issues on your own and through family discussions. However, when you have faced significant trauma, have developed an extremely unhealthy form of attachment style, and display attachment behavior that is damaging to yourself and others, you may need to find a professional such as an EFFT therapist to help you. This person is specifically trained to guide you through the process of developing healthier attachment styles and foster positive behavior and thinking mindsets.

Within the U.S. (and abroad), you can find a registered therapist or support center by logging onto the International Center for Excellence in Emotional Family Therapy (ICEEFT) at https://iceeft.com where you can learn more about EFFT, find therapists, become a therapist, and find additional support.

Chapter 4:

Cognitive Behavioral

Therapy and Self-

Improvement

Image 6: Julie Rose from Pixabay. We all carry a suitcase with us through life. It is filled with our experiences and it can determine how we act. When that suitcase is overloaded with things we choose not to think about, we become clumsy and

burdened in life. Only when we open the suitcase and unpack our experiences can we begin to lighten our load and step forward with intention and purpose.

What Is Cognitive Behavioral Therapy (CBT)?

CBT consists of many techniques, strategies, and interventions that can be used on a daily basis to help foster self-reflection, build self-esteem, and facilitate communication. It also helps with conflict resolution and finding healthy ways to express emotions. It is an effective therapy to help with the reframing of your current attachment style as the ultimate goal of the strategies and techniques are to foster a healthy and secure sense of self. This, in turn, creates a healthy secure attachment style.

In essence, CBT is talk therapy. It is about finding ways to talk about your feelings, your thoughts, and the way in which you tend to behave in certain situations. CBT is geared towards finding thinking patterns and the resulting emotions that are negative and unhelpful. The ultimate goal of CBT is to help people see how their current way of thinking and doing things results in negative emotions. It then helps them train their thoughts to be logical and positive, creating behavior that is constructive and stable, which enables them to feel contentment, satisfaction, and discover inner peace.

In the end, our thinking, actions, and feelings are all related in a transactional exchange. Therefore, when you change one component, you change the outcome. Changing your thinking will change your behavior and your feelings.

This transaction can be visualized in the following example:

you are not enough	you withdrawing from responsibilities	you feel depressed
Thinking	Behavior	Feeling

How CBT Is Used to Treat Anxiety and Depression Disorders

CBT is highly effective in treating anxiety and depression disorders (Helpguide, n.d.). It focuses on identifying the stressor that influences your thinking, analyzing what you are thinking, and finding ways to change that thought so you will behave differently when in a similar situation in future, thereby feeling better about your ability to deal with a stressor. As example: You feel uncomfortable when you go to a party with a friend (social anxiety disorder), and you panic about the party beforehand. As a result, you become anxious, avoid taking the friend's calls, and eventually feel like you have failed that friend. When you are invited to another party in future, you will recall this incident and feel even worse, therefore, acting in an even more negative way.

So, how do you break this cycle? With CBT, you are encouraged to think about what the problem may be. Perhaps you have an instigating incident or early trauma relating to a party, which is holding you back from enjoying social activities with your friend in the future? Alternatively, you may fear rejection when in a crowd, and this could lead to your negative feelings. CBT would help you to discover the root cause of your thinking, which influences your behavior and your feelings. Therefore, the basic tenet of CBT is that people's thinking about situations is what influences their behavior and feelings. It is not a specific event that influences how we act; it's how we think about that event.

CBT: The Process

The process of CBT is to evaluate thinking patterns, find negative patterns, and replace these with positive ones. With the help of a therapist, you can identify the thinking issues that affect your life in a negative or limiting manner, and you can then create a strategy for dealing with these. Basically, you learn to discover faulty logic and inappropriate or unsatisfactory emotional responses. This process allows you to work on your actions and modify your beliefs.

If we continue with the earlier example of being invited to a party, your thinking might be evaluated as follow:

Negative thought one: I am not popular at parties, so I shouldn't go.

Illogical reasoning: You are jumping to a conclusion, and there's no evidence to support this.

Logical reasoning: If you do go and don't enjoy it, you can always leave earlier.

Negative thought two: I always feel awkward at parties and make a fool of myself.

Illogical reasoning: You are generalizing based on one bad experience in the past.

Logical reasoning: This time could be different, and you might enjoy your time there.

Negative thought three: Parties are filled with drugs, criminals, and they do bad things there.

Illogical reasoning: You are seeing it only in negative terms. This is not how reality works.

Logical reasoning: Parties may have some of those influences, but there are also good people there whom you can relate to.

This reasoning process reveals another basic tenet of CBT—we all have distorted thinking we subscribe to. These thinking patterns are not based on logic but have rather formed from our own negative experiences.

When we surrender our thinking to these distortions, we will begin to engage in attachment styles that support our negative thoughts. What you think, you manifest. How you behave will affect your thoughts, and this can create a negative cycle that spirals ever deeper into unhealthy attachments and behavior. As negative thinking becomes your norm, you will manifest unhealthy behavior styles such as anxious and anxious-avoidant styles of behavior. This, in turn, could lead to associated problems such as depression, anxiety disorders, addictions, phobias, panic disorders, and personality disorders. It is important to discover your thinking flaws or negative thinking styles to improve your behavior attachments and subsequent emotional reactions.

Common Types of Cognitive Distortions Based on Your Attachment Style

Image 7: Rostyslav Savchyn on Unsplash. Cognitive distortions are like looking at the world through the filters of a kaleidoscope, and it can severely affect your logical perspective. While you may firmly believe something to be a certain way, you merely perceive it as such due to your flawed thinking patterns. Once you learn to discard negative and faulty logic, your whole world can change for the better.

There are a range of thinking or cognitive distortions that can influence your behavior style. Each of these distortions, in part, originates from a past experience or by faulty reasoning that has become your way of thinking. While you may not believe your brain has the power to improve your life (and it does), it certainly can ruin your life (when you use it in a flawed way).

Here are some popular ways people engage in distorted thinking pathways and how to counter this:

- **Always Being Right**

While we all want to be right, and being wrong can be an embarrassment, expecting to be right the whole time is illogical. When this form of thinking becomes your norm, you may start engaging in anxiety-driven behavior when you are proven wrong in a situation. You lack the ability to then see things from someone else's point of view, and you have developed an over-dependence on yourself and your "superior" status as being right the whole time. This arrogant thinking will cut you off from the emotions of others, and even your own emotions will become a confused entanglement as you shift between feelings of pride and feelings of despair.

As the joke goes, "I found Mr. Right, but I didn't know his first name is Always." This does not only apply to men though, and being right the whole time is not only a pain to the people around you, but it can also end up being exhausting and isolating to you.

Countering It: To beat something you are secretly scared of, it may be helpful to intentionally do it. Like someone who is scared of heights who climbs tall buildings to become less scared, you can choose to intentionally do something wrong, such as giving an incorrect answer to a question. This experience should allow you to begin adjusting to being incorrect and accept that you are not always right, and with practice, you will be okay when you are wrong.

- **Black-and-White or Polarized Thinking**

People who only see the world in terms of it being black or white tend to have polarized thinking where they can only see one thing as being right and everything else as being wrong. Life, as we mostly find, is composed of shades of gray, and what is right for one person will not be right for you. This is a normal perspective. However, when you believe the other person to be wrong, no matter their circumstances, this becomes flawed or illogical thinking. Often, this form of thinking combines with the notion of yourself always being right.

As a result, this causes great anxiety in your mind as you try to survive in a world that does not seem to agree with your norms. This can again lead to dissociation and isolation. It is instinctive to withdraw from what we see as threatening our way of thinking. In extreme cases, this form of isolating thinking can lead to the formation of cults and extremist thinking.

Countering It: People who tend towards polarized thinking will not step outside their comfort zone, and they struggle with new ideas as this makes them question where they stand on something. Therefore, engaging with new ideas, going to new places, and visiting strange cultures can be a great way to break down these preconceptions. Joining online chat rooms to discuss how people think and feel can also help to widen your perspectives and modulate your narrow view of the world. Should you choose to do this, you would need to become aware of any judgments you have about the conversations or topics being discussed. This will help alert you to your polarized thinking. Once you know you are doing it, you can begin to watch out for these illogical measures in the future.

- **Negative Filtering**

We all have personality types, and being a negative Neil is certainly more common than you might think. There are some people who simply see the world through a negative filter. Regardless of the type of situation or what is actually going on, they see it as being negative and believe it will harm them, so they avoid it, and even then they feel negative about that action too. This is an extreme form of pessimism.

Oftentimes, this form of thinking is "inherited" from a parent who displayed this form of thinking distortion. It can also form as a result of a negative or disappointing event or experience that has so devastated you that you simply can't see the world with a positive eye again. Sadly, this results in instability and unhealthy attachment formation. You will doubt others so will avoid them. You will also doubt yourself, so you will self-isolate and avoid thinking about yourself, which leads to a low self-esteem and reduces your relationship satisfaction. After all, how can you be in a satisfying relationship when you see the world, your partner, and your interactions as being bad?

Countering It: Individuals with this distorted way of thinking need to be consciously reminded of the positivity in life. This does not mean you should wrap them in cotton wool and sing them lullabies the whole time. Instead, they should practice being positive, showing gratitude, and make an effort to eliminate their negative thinking. Starting with awareness of self-talk and thoughts can be really useful. Keeping a gratitude journal, writing down their thoughts, and coloring them according to emotions (red for negative, green for positive), they can begin to visualize their thoughts changing as they consciously think happy or positive thoughts. Even wearing an elastic band on your wrist and snapping it whenever you have a negative thought or a negative reaction to something that you begin to realize is not negative is a great way to retrain your thinking.

- **Catastrophizing**

This form of distorted thinking is the proverbial waiting for the sword of Damocles to drop. You anticipate that something bad will happen as a result of something insignificant. Perhaps this originated from being punished too severely as a child or being told you were not good enough while growing up, but now it persists as an adult, and you think you suck, so you look for things you can fail at—and it will be the end of the world to you!

Even something as insignificant as dropping your boss' files at work will have you convinced that punishment (and hellfire) will follow. Surely, you will lose your job as a result of this heinous crime? And even when someone praises you for doing something right, you still look for ways to minimize their praise or negate your praiseworthiness. You might say things like "Oh, no! It was a team effort" or "I really didn't do much."

As a result of believing and looking for the worst to happen, you don't trust the world or the people in it. You are like a child waiting to be punished for kicking out the neighbor's window. This fills you with anxiety and drains all the pleasure and wonder out of life. You are constantly traumatized, and you quite likely have a depressive personality type as a result.

Countering It: You need to learn to accept praise. Give it to yourself; you need it. Keep a positivity journal in which you write down all the good things you have done every day. Create your own support group of people who build you up and can validate your daily successes with an honest opinion and also help you realize that the thing you think is the end of the world is not all that bad (if it's even anything at all). In all likelihood, you are a worrier, someone who battles their own worry demons each day. You need confirmation that your worries are unfounded.

• Singular Blame

With this distorted thinking, you are an either-or person. You either think you are to blame for everything, or you believe the world is to blame for everything. Neither of these thinking paradigms is correct though. When you have a balanced life view, you accept that sometimes you are to blame, such as burning the supper because you were texting on your phone and not paying attention. At other times, the world or outside forces are to blame, such as burning the supper because you had to help your neighbor who was having a heart attack.

Many times, this distorted thinking results from being overly criticized as a child or from some childhood trauma like an overly zealous religious event (or doctrine) you were not mentally prepared for (and you now think you are destined to suffer; hence, you feel you are to blame).

The opposite holds true when you feel you have no control over your life. You have come to believe that you can take no action to influence what happens, so you don't. This can create disinterested behavior and a low self-esteem. Relating to others becomes a problem since you take no responsibility, and you can't be counted on.

Countering It: Therapeutic interventions may be required here, and you would benefit from being professionally guided towards developing an understanding that the world does not hinge on your decisions, so it's okay to fail sometimes. Nor can the world run when you are not participating and take no responsibility for your actions. You need to own up when you are to blame and step back when it's simply circumstances.

Journaling can certainly help as it will make you aware of what your self-talk sounds like and guide your thoughts towards more neutral territory.

- **Fallacy of Fairness**

The world is not fair. How often have we heard that being said? People often hide behind it when they think the world has turned against them. Reality: the world simply is. Fairness has nothing to do with it. True, we get injustices such as crime and inequalities, but again, fairness does not really apply to it. When someone robs you, it is not because they want to be unfair. It is probably because they need money, or they have been living a life of crime and know no different. When a colleague at work gets a promotion, and you don't, this is not an example of unfairness. Rather, it simply means that your colleague was better placed to be promoted. Things go our way one day, and they go against us the next day. Fairness has little to do with it.

When you believe the world should be fair to you, it sets you up for extreme disappointment and disillusionment. When you then decide the world is not fair because you have been disappointed, this negatively influences your thinking, which affects future events beyond the "unfair" event.

Countering It: Learning to let go of the concept of being fair or not is often learned through techniques such as meditation. Instead of focusing on the world outside and potential negative events, you learn to focus on simplistic concepts that are neither fair nor unfair, such as breathing, body awareness, and releasing bad memories.

- **Over-Generalization**

This is fallacious thinking based on one negative event in the past informing all of your decision-making skills. For instance, being robbed by someone who is African American could lead you to conclude that all African Americans are criminals. Clearly, this is not factual or logical thinking (criminals come in all colors and nationalities). Even something as simple as being disappointed by one faulty car, which makes you refuse to drive that kind of car again is an example of this. As shown by the first example, over-generalization can create substantially negative thinking and behavior patterns. It is an unbalanced way to go through life, and it will severely limit your chances and options in life.

Countering It: Play the devil's advocate. When you are given to generalization, you can use the approach of being "against" your view to help you become more balanced in your thinking. It's about putting yourself in the other person's shoes or seeing a situation from the other side. You can do this as a journaling activity. So, when you have come to generalize that all blondes are dumb, as an example, find reasons to counter this belief. You could remind yourself that hair color has nothing to do with intellectual facility. If you believe you suck at job interviews, you could remind yourself of all the times you have had a successful conversation with someone new, and how this is precisely what a job interview is.

- **Assumptive Thinking**

We tend to make assumptions easily. It is really when we are too lazy to think things through. We rely on what we think we know and jump to a conclusion about something or someone. This is the normal end of the spectrum for most of us; however, when you jump to conclusions about everything without any evidence, this is distorted thinking and decision making at play. This can manifest as a "gut feeling" that someone doesn't like us, or they are out to get us, or that we didn't make a good impression on someone (all without having any facts to substantiate this logic).

With this kind of unsubstantiated thinking, it is very easy to become detached from reality and develop a mistrust of people in your life. You might develop a behavior style that is anxiety driven or feel ambivalent about people in general, making real connections virtually impossible.

Counter It: To counter this distorted thinking, you need to become like a scientist. Whatever you believe, you should support it with evidence. If you believe someone doesn't like you, then don't allow this belief without concrete evidence, such as them telling someone they don't like you. Basing your assumption on "a look" is not evidence enough. While gut feelings can help us out, they should not govern our actions in everything in life.

- **Emotional Reasoning**

This distorted thinking revolves around feeling something and believing it to be true. You feel bloated, so you believe you are fat. You feel unhappy, so you believe you are depressed. While your feelings are important, they are not supposed to dominate your thinking. Feelings can't reason, and they can't be logical. Being overly determined by your feelings can lead to unhealthy behavior habits such as anxiety-driven attachments. It also prevents you from seeing the world as it is, and not as you feel about it.

Counter It: Emotions can be tricky to balance, and you may need professional intervention such as EFFT. A trained therapist can help you make healthy associations based on your feelings and also help you discover how to control your emotions, instead of letting them control you. Journaling and using positive affirmations can also help you to find healthy self-expression, while meditation can help you acknowledge and release potentially harmful emotions that have no factual reason to influence your being.

• Blaming

As children, we often tend to use this form of behavior to get out of trouble. Mom asks who broke the plate, and we all point at our younger brother, hoping to avoid punishment. Sadly, this kind of thinking still persists into adulthood for many people. When they are faced with possible punishment, they are quick to place the blame on someone who may not even be involved in the issue. We even end up blaming someone for the way we feel or for what we do. When a wife blames her infidelity on her husband's inattentiveness, this is a form of fallacious thinking. Clearly, the husband did not strip her and throw her into another man's bed. Though his inattention is not healthy, it is not what forced the wife to act as she did.

We are responsible for our actions. Therefore, we can't assign blame to others and state they made us do something. To do so is an example of distorted thinking.

Counter It: Start using words of power to help focus your thinking on you and not on the people around you. For instance, when you want to blame someone for making you swear, you should say, "I chose to swear." If you believe someone made or caused you to miss your bus, you can say, "I alone missed the bus." Consciously take ownership of your thinking and actions.

● Rule-Based Thinking

Many of us develop rules that seem to govern how we live and what makes us feel comfortable. For instance, we may believe that women should be soft and feminine. When we are then faced by the image of a female bodybuilder, this challenges our rule-based thinking, and we may end up being rude to that woman as we are inevitably angry as she didn't follow our rules. This is also about seeing the world as we want it (and have ordained it) to be. But we are not the kings and queens of the earth. The world does not operate according to our rules.

Any thinking that removes you from interacting with what is real and there in your environment creates behavior based on distortions. It will lead to withdrawal, emotional instability, and difficulty accepting and trusting the world, which creates anxiety-driven behavior styles.

Counter It: When little children learn, they often drive us nuts by asking "why?" This is actually a good thing as you need to explain, and therefore, think about something. Hence, when you feel upset as something seems "wrong" to you, you should start asking yourself "why?" When you see a same-sex couple together and it pushes on one of your personal life rules (or your fallacious thinking), ask yourself why you think it is wrong. When you can't answer it in a satisfactory manner, you start to question your fallacious beliefs and can begin to see the world as it is.

• Self-Sacrifice as Reward

Many of us have come to expect that sacrifice brings reward, and this is often not the case. This kind of distorted thinking only brings disappointment and resentment when we do something with an expectation of reward only to receive nothing in return. This is also an example of the world not reacting as we expect, which causes confusion and let-down with us. Accepting that the world will not necessarily reward your sacrifices with bounty or feast will help you to adjust better by forming a secure attachment style.

Counter It: If you enjoy engaging in sacrificial behavior, it may be healthier to satisfy that need by engaging in charity work where there is no promise of return. This way, you will learn you can't influence what other people do or how they return favors.

Self-Improvement Practices and Exercises

Image 8: Hannah Olinger on Unsplash. Self-improvement practices and exercises can include constructive tasks like journaling and meditation or it can include more challenging tasks such as guided discovery journeys. The goal is to experience the emotion or behavior you want to change and then plot how you will go about changing this negative or unhelpful behavior. This plot includes how you will change it, to what you will change it, and how you will feel in the end.

- **Journaling**

This is a little different from a usual journal or diary in that the sole purpose is to capture and gather information about your emotions or feelings, your thinking patterns, and your actions or behavior. This is a great tool to use for self-development as it allows you to tangibly look at your thoughts, behavior, and feelings. When it is made tangible on paper, you will find it easier to start reflecting on possible solutions. It is also useful for evaluating the progress you make as you start trying out different solutions.

In your journal, you can use activities such as word associations, mind maps, and even image-based reflections to help you articulate how you feel, why you feel that way, and what you are going to do about it. Thanks to technology, there are even apps for this now, with several well-rated apps available online. The CBT Tools for Healthy Living, Self-Help Mood Diary by *Excel At Life* is available for download to most mobile devices from Google Play Store and can be downloaded free at https://play.google.com/store/apps/details?id=com.ex celatlife.cbtdiary&hl=en_ZA while Apple users can download a similar online product called CBT Thought Diary from Eddie Liu at https://apps.apple.com/us/app/cbt-thought-diary/id1010391170.

• Meditation

Meditation as a daily practice, not a once-off fad, is very useful for de-stressing and developing a peaceful mindset. There are various techniques and styles for meditation, and you can certainly find a way that works for you. From simply listening to a guided meditation to participating in specific breathing exercises, there are many different approaches. Guided meditations can be found free on YouTube, and there are several channels dedicated exclusively to this, such as *Meditation Vacation* or *Jason Stephenson's channel* that has an assortment of highly popular guided meditations on.

A similar skill that may help you release tension and bring inner peace is taking up a practice such as tai chi, which is like moving meditation. The goal here is to give your stressed brain a break, allow your body to become grounded, and find a more peaceful way to think. If you are anxious-avoidant in your normal behavior, you will find it holds less power over you when you can reduce your anxiety, opening up your mind to think with greater clarity and perspective.

• Cognitive Restructuring or Reframing

Using the journaling you have started doing and the peaceful mindful state of meditation, you can begin to explore your perceptions and beliefs, not only finding and challenging negative ones, but also finding healthy thoughts to replace them with. For instance, if you believe a woman is only as good as the family she creates, but you suddenly undergo a divorce, you may find your negative thoughts are challenged. Instead of only trying to believe a woman is not only her family, you might begin to question yourself what it is that makes a woman.

- **Guided Discovery**

Sometimes we believe things without knowing why we believe them or how we came to believe them. These thoughts are not always negative, but in not knowing where these thoughts came from, you will not be able to embrace your mind's processes. Using your journal and perhaps the help of a counselor, you can begin to find evidence to support your beliefs or assumptions. So, if you believe you have no right to speak in public, you would need to find evidence for that belief. In some countries, this is an actual law, but when considering it in line with your own legal concepts, you might find your evidence does disprove your thinking.

- **Exposure/Desensitizing Therapy**

Anxiety can give rise to a range of behavior that is not beneficial to your health or well-being. Exposure or desensitizing therapy can be really helpful in dealing with negative behavior and mindsets such as phobias, fears, and anxiety triggers. It works on the principle of starting with small exposure to the thing that scares or triggers you. The exposure is short, and afterwards, you discuss how you felt with a therapist. The next day, you may experience the same length of exposure again; this time, you are encouraged to remain calm and not panic. When you feel less frightened or upset over the experience, you will face longer incremental exposure to the trigger.

In reality, if you are terrified of spiders, you may start by looking at a picture of a spider for a few minutes and then discussing how you felt. You might journal about the experience, how it made your skin crawl, and how it made your brain feel numb. The following day, you may have to hold the photo, then next time, you may have to watch a video of a spider moving on someone's hand. Eventually, this would culminate with you going to a petting zoo to have an actual spider walk on your hand too.

With gradually increasing exposure, you begin to feel confident in your ability to handle the emotions of this fearful experience. You are able to analyze how and what you think, which, in turn, influences your actions. Anxiety can be controlled, which opens the road to secure attachment and thinking styles.

- **Activity Scheduling**

Your calendar can be your friend. Sometimes, we have an activity we are not really eager to do as it is in some way linked to having to face a fear or engage with an anxiety trigger. Going to the dentist is for many people a fine example of this. Using your calendar, you can begin to mentally prepare yourself for the activity, while you resolutely refuse to postpone the activity. Once your appointment is set, you can begin to stop focusing on it and rather deal with it on the day when you need to go for the appointment.

• De-Stressing Techniques

Anxiety has a biological component too. It affects not only how you feel; it also influences your rate of respiration, blood pressure, heart rate, and even your perspiration. We certainly know when we are anxious we get sweaty palms, and some people even complain of stomach difficulties from prolonged periods of anxiety. To bring some relief on a physical level, you are encouraged to try the following techniques:

Breathing Relaxation: This has already been somewhat introduced to you in meditation; however, there are a range of breathing techniques you may consider. Box breathing has become very popular recently (and not only because it's being used by law enforcement officers and Navy SEALs). In essence, it is symmetrical breathing, and it is very easy to do. When you find yourself in an anxiety-fueled situation, you can benefit by doing it right there. Breathing in through your nose for four seconds, you pause for four seconds, then exhale through your mouth for four seconds, followed by another pause for four seconds to complete one set. Quite simply, it's inhale (four seconds), hold (four seconds), exhale (four seconds), hold (four seconds), and begin again.

Breathing creates mindfulness, lowers your blood pressure, encourages slow deep heart activity, and it even lowers your temperature (no more sweaty palms). When your blood is more oxygenated, you will be able to think more clearly and feel less anxious.

Progressive Body Scan: Like the breathing exercises and meditation, a progressive body scan notes the physical cost of constant anxiety and worry. As you mentally become aware of every part of your body, you note tension, pain, tightness, and discomfort. Using the focus of your intention, you can begin to gently tighten and release muscles, banish pain, and relax your body as you begin to let anxiety go.

- **Role Playing**

As the name states, this is about playing out roles to find new insight and acceptance of what happens in your life. Fear-inducing scenarios become less scary as you develop problem-solving skills, become familiar with new circumstances and gain insight, develop social skills and become more assertive in what you need and want, and you learn to communicate better. This is an effective way to engage in examples of the devil's advocate role play where you reason on behalf of someone else.

Chapter 5:

Finding Happiness in Your

Single Life

Image 9: Priscilla Du Preez on Unsplash. Being single is a daunting experience for many of us. We desperately want to be in a relationship, forgetting that relationships are definitely not an easy road to walk, and these come with their own challenges.

Being happily single is becoming a buzz concept of late, and more young people are choosing to remain single or embrace being single once their current relationships have ended. So, what does it take to find happiness in your singlehood?

Your Attachment Style and Your Confidence

While you may want to be in a happy relationship, the first relationship you will ever have is with yourself. It is essential to discover happiness in this primary relationship, for it is one you will remain a part of for the rest of your life. Being single and happy with your singlehood is a number one factor for avoiding toxic relationships with partners who are simply available but not suitable for you. Once you know what you are looking for, you will have no issues in maintaining healthy boundaries between you and your partner, and between your relationship and the outside world. This is how you ensure the relationship remains a happy place to live, and stop it from becoming a traumatic war zone.

If you have already developed an insecure or harmful attachment style, this does not mean you are doomed to constantly be unhappy in your relationships. It simply means you have some obstacles to overcome, which might translate into a longer journey to reaching your ideal relationship status.

When you have formed anxious or dependent attachment behavior styles, you will struggle with being on your own. This imposes restrictions on the relationship, and your partner now has to haul your life baggage around with them too. Not everyone is cut out for this, nor need they be. This is your battle to fight. You need to decide what you will leave behind, and what you will take with you.

While you may be looking for a partner who lifts you up, and you may be fortunate enough to find a partner who is willing to do just that, this will be a temporary fix. You can't place your happiness in someone else's hands. That's like expecting to find happiness in a commercially available form to consume when you want it—like eating a lollipop and instantly feeling better. It won't last.

Only *you* can make yourself rise and feel lifted.

After searching for numerous partners and being in one failed relationship after another, you may have become quite skeptical of real love really existing. As a result, you may settle for a relationship that may not be right for you, but it's convenient and right there.

Eventually, you start accepting things you shouldn't. You may stick with a partner who cheats on you because at least he doesn't beat you. Perhaps you accept a wife who doesn't love you and who becomes emotionally abusive because you have children with her whom you adore.

This settling "down" will not end happily in the long run. While this does not mean you need to bail out of the relationship right now, it may mean you need to begin traveling along the therapeutic road to see if you can create a relationship that all the people involved in can enjoy and feel satisfied with.

What You Want From a Relationship, You Want From Yourself

You may have been asked what you want from a relationship, and many of us are quick to list the following conditions:

- Stability
- Love
- Care
- Affection
- Protection
- Support
- Happiness
- Family

These certainly seem like the best qualities in life and having all these conditions met would probably create a holy-grail kind of relationship. While your list may look slightly different, the basic principles will be the same. But, here's the kicker: these relationship goals can apply to your singlehood or relationship with self too. If you can't create these conditions in yourself, how can you offer them to someone else? You are expecting it from your partner, but if they don't already have this in them, they can't share it with you. Likewise, if you don't have this in you, then you can't share it or share in it either.

When you can safely and confidently create these conditions in your relationship with yourself, you will not be dependent on someone else for contentment or happiness. You will also be able to share these qualities with your partner, becoming the ideal partner for your ideal partner. Remember: a relationship takes two people (more when you start having children), and when you are already unhappy, you will not bring anything except unhappiness to your relationship. So, engage in and grow from activities on your own to help you become stable, loving, caring, affectionate, protective, supportive, happy, and family to *yourself*.

Challenges to Overcome

Embracing your singlehood is certainly not going to be easy. There will be many challenges to overcome in addition to the process of becoming all of the above requirements you created. These challenges include:

- ## Social Stigma of Being Single

Choosing to remain single is not condoned, accepted, or understood in most societies on earth. There is the constant social pressure to become a part of a relationship unit, continue the bloodline, family name, and have children. Perhaps you may be fortunate enough that some of your family members will understand and accept your singlehood decision, but many of them will not. This means that family gatherings will usually involve the inevitable, "When are you getting married?"

Society also tends to tie age to this concept, and when you are nearing a certain age, the pressures to commit to a relationship usually build. This can push you towards entering into a relationship without being ready or even if the relationship is not suitable for your needs.

Remind yourself daily that being single is not something to apologize for, nor is it something to be ashamed of. Whether you choose to remain single forever, or you choose to enter a relationship, the goals will remain the same. However, if you can satisfy those goals in your selfhood, you are more likely to be able to have a satisfactory relationship with another unique individual.

- ## Your Own Neediness

We all like to feel validated, to have our existence and our experiences witnessed by another person. This can create pressure to enter a relationship to get this outside validation. However, you do not need to rely on a partner or significant other to get this validation. Even a close friend or someone you trust can act in this capacity, assuring and confirming that you are on the right track and you are doing things right.

In reality, you might get more validation from a close friend than from your relationship partner. Affirmation and positive feedback is more likely to come from a dear friend than from a lover, husband, or wife who is not involved or invested enough to meet and satisfy your neediness.

- **Relationship Urges**

We live in a society that is geared towards couples, and this can make things difficult for singles to feel accepted and happy. Going out can become problematic when you are on your own. Eating out, going to a movie, clubbing, and attending shows becomes awkward when you are without company. Certainly, the "couples discounts" and "family buckets" clearly indicate which way society is inclined. Again, this can lead to alienation and loneliness when you are still trying to find your own power in a singlehood.

These can all increase the urge to join a relationship simply to not be alone. This is, of course, not the right reason to enter into a relationship. Again, you would be placing your happiness in someone else's hands, and when they can't meet your needs, you open the door to resentment. Compromising by entering a relationship before you are ready will not lead to the happily ever-after you are dreaming of.

- **Self-Confidence Issues**

Over time, especially as your friends get married and have children, you will begin to doubt the wisdom of your decision to self-develop in your singlehood. You may begin to lose self-confidence, and you will wonder if you have waited too long. Perhaps your partner has already come and gone? With aging factoring in, you may begin to feel as if you are not good enough, pretty enough, young enough, or simply enough to attract a partner. This could also prompt you to settle for the first possible relationship that comes along. Again, you have not ensured your happiness; instead, you have placed your happiness in someone else's hands. It belongs in your hands, and the right partner for yourself is you. Once you are happily single, you will be a perfect partner for the right partner.

Singlehood Models

Your attachment style is a valuable motivating factor in being single (Brenner, 2018). Insecure forms of attachment are statistically linked to a lesser chance of being single as you struggle with being alone, while it is also linked to a higher chance of being in a relationship that is unhappy. The secure attachment style is most associated with being happily single, or happy in a stable relationship. People who are prone to anxious attachment styles tend to become single not by choice but because partners leave them or they struggle to secure a partner.

Singlehood can be a choice, and most often, those who choose to be single do so from a secure attachment style. These individuals have the confidence to do so. However, when considering the three models that lead to or create singlehood, we find the following:

- **Anxious and Activated**

People who default to anxious attachment styles tend to make poor partners in a relationship. While they seek intimacy, once they have this in a relationship, they tend to become hyperactivated, a condition where their behavior kicks into overdrive. Where they were anxious before, they become neurotic; where they were fearful of being abandoned, they now become jealous and controlling of their partner. Needless to say, the relationship becomes unbalanced, and often the only option open to the relationship is its end, with the anxious styled partner being forced into singlehood.

- **Avoidant**

Individuals who have an avoidant attachment style tend to believe being within the bounds of a relationship will end in unhappiness and pain. They view the intimacy of a relationship with trepidation, and they fear being close to people and revealing their vulnerability. As a result, such individuals tend to naturally choose singlehood not out of any reason other than they fear being in a relationship. Singlehood does not offer them joy or contentment, as they are simply hiding in it from their own hang-ups.

When these people are in a relationship, they maintain a foot-out-the-door philosophy, being ready to leave and flee to the unattached nature of being single. They tend to be aloof, unaffectionate, and disinterested, causing their relationships to fail. Avoidant typed people will also not easily enter another relationship again, preferring to remain single, even though it does not necessarily meet their needs either.

- **Single, Secure, and Happy**

With increasing frequency, as societal norms are being challenged and broken down, we find individuals who have a secure attachment style, who choose to remain or enter singlehood. These are people who can happily meet all their needs from a range of non-romantic relationships, and even their sexual needs, if they have them, are met outside of a romantic relationship.

The reasons for being single may include spiritual, religious, or a heightened need for space to engage in self-discovery and development. While these people would make excellent partners in a romantic relationship, they choose not to necessarily engage in a romantic relationship, instead forming lasting and satisfying bonds with themselves. This choice is also not driven by some buried childhood trauma or anxious avoidance; rather, it is a conscious and carefully considered choice.

How to Become Single, Secure, and Happy

More and more people are choosing singlehood as a permanent lifestyle choice; however, some choose to combine it with a therapeutic treatment to find, care for, and develop their own selves and create healthier attachment styles. In these cases, it can be considered an intermediary stage between an unhappy relationship and finding a satisfactory relationship when they are ready. Whichever your choice for being or becoming single, your happiness and satisfaction is in your hands, which requires you to develop or maintain a secure attachment style:

- **Mindfulness Techniques**

When you are ready to engage in developing yourself, you will need to start a process of finding yourself, consciously identifying the root causes of your insecurities, and actively repair your insecurities. Using methods such as meditation, journaling, and therapy you will be able to start finding out who you are, what happened to you, what you need, and how to give that to yourself instead of looking for it elsewhere.

This is not an instant fix, and humming while you sit in the lotus position will not quickly make everything better. Instead, it is a life-long commitment to yourself. It is like admitting you have a preexisting condition that you need to nurture and take care of for the rest of your life. You can choose to ignore it and hope for the best, or you can be proactive and learn to cope with and adapt to your behavior style, making it become as close to confident and secure as you can.

Creating healthy self-care and self-soothing routines such as daily journaling, reflection, mindfulness through meditation, breathing exercises, and intentionally facing your fears, you will be able to be the best possible version of yourself, the most secure you that you can be, and you will find a state of contentment with yourself (and eventually in a suitable relationship if you so choose).

Even if you already come from a stable background, have suffered no past traumas, and you are very secure in who you are, creating mindful routines of self-care to practice daily will help you remain secure in the face of daily pressures and challenges.

• Therapy and Relationship Counseling

Okay, so you have some issues that you need to deal with before you can securely enter a new relationship. This is not the end of the world, but if you are not proactive, it can be the end of yet another relationship. If you don't become responsible enough to admit you need help, you may even further damage your relationship with yourself.

Going for therapy or signing up for relationship counseling need not be an admission of defeat. There is no shame in needing help. In fact, you should be applauded for being brave enough to do it. The benefits of having therapy to help you face your troubled past, and finding out what you want, or making sense of your own tumbled thoughts is immeasurable. You will become stronger, wiser, and much more confident in who you are on your own and who you are in a relationship. How is that not a win-win situation for you?

Relationship counseling will not only assist you in finding out how to make your existing relationship work, and discover what you actually want from a relationship, but it will also help improve your relationship with yourself. Remember, your relationship partner is not there to fix you. And you are not there to fix them, either. A healthy, satisfying, and dependable relationship is about being together, facing outside (and inside) challenges together while being dependable enough to be counted on. When you build that relationship with yourself first, you will be ready to engage in the challenges of two independent and secure people becoming a unity in the relationship. Entering a relationship with a partner who is not secure in their attachments brings with it a whole range of complications. You are not their savior.

You should not engage in a relationship bearing a messiah complex, for then you are not able to help someone out at all. Instead, you can point them in a direction to engage in self-development, support them through the healing process, and then see if the relationship will work. A trained therapist can help you in this regard, assisting you to steer clear of pity pitfalls and traps of dependent anxiety your partner may already be creating for you (usually quite unintentionally on their part).

- **Analyze Your Needs and Wants**

What you need and what you want is not always clear, especially in the technological age, where the media is constantly telling us what to think, how to be, and what we need or want. However, looking back at your past relationships, what strikes you as being an obvious need (that was probably not met) or a want (that you had satisfied or not). A previous partner may have been domineering, and now you know you do not want this.

Perhaps they were caring, which you enjoyed, and you want this. Maybe the lines of communication were not available to you during the relationship, and you missed being able to simply talk to them. Even non-romantic relationships can help you find out what you enjoy and don't. Camaraderie, sharing, talking, caring, respect and trust, intimacy, sex, and friendship may be on your list of things you need and want. Surprisingly, you can satisfy these needs in non-romantic relationships, or even with yourself. When you know how to tend to your own needs, you will know what you expect from and need from your partner.

Take some time to journal about this. Write about past relationships, even relationships that didn't involve you, such as that of your parents, siblings, friends, or colleagues and find the things that stuck out to you as being something you would want and need. Having a partner who walks into your office and tongues you down to your toes is not a healthy or viable need. If this is something you believe you need, you may need to dig a little deeper as there is an insecurity you are not dealing with. However, wanting a partner who sends you a daily message with kind wishes and shows their affection by talking to you and discussing how they can help you build your relationship is a secure and positive need.

- **Engage in Meaningful Activities**

Happiness is determined more by your feeling about an activity than who you necessarily do it with (if anyone). Enjoyment comes from doing something that matters to you. Find what gets you excited, passionate, and interested and go do it. Whether it's going on a weekly hike, taking up sky-diving, or simply browsing the local flower shops every weekend to make yourself a beautiful bouquet for the week, you can enjoy and find personal meaning on your own. When you are happy, you will also have a greater chance at attracting someone who is like-minded and secure in their attachment style.

- **Supporting People**

While you are busy journaling, take some time to really think about the people in your life. Are they helping or hurting you? Often, we attract people into our lives with the best intentions only to find they are not helpful to our personal journey. They may be emotional leeches, they may be dominators, or even secretly frenemies who are only waiting for you to fail so they can rejoice. You may also be blessed with dear friends who support you when you need it; people who care enough to either voice an opinion or keep quiet and be exactly what you need in the right moment.

Having a strong support circle is important when you engage in a selfhood relationship. You are not planning on being a hermit (hopefully), and you will need people to meet your needs to communicate, share ideas with, spend time with, develop friendship with, laugh with, and turn to when you are having a bad day, or needing assurance and validation. Choose people who help (not hurt), people who care and don't scare, and people who support you with no ulterior motives. You are worth it.

- **Live Now**

Don't be a one-day person. Someone who has all these great plans of what they will do when they are in a relationship, but then wait for that relationship to happen. These one-day people are living in a dream of one-day. What about today?

If you are planning to take a trip, then do so, whether you are single or not. Don't wait until you find a partner. Live now. Find ways to satisfy your life goals now and don't wait for someone else to make it happen for you. You are all you need.

- **Stop Speed Dating**

If you are busy working on creating a better selfhood, or making yourself into the best version of yourself, you may be tempted to start dating before you are ready. This can be overwhelming, and it can really knock you back from all the good progress you have made. Instead, wait a bit longer until you are ready to date again. Don't allow society or anyone else to push you into meeting someone because they are "nice" or because you are simply "available." You are already dating someone—yourself. And that is the best relationship you should be focused on until you are ready to step back into dating and then only *if* you want to.

- **Declutter Your Mind**

Become mindful of your thoughts. What you think will influence your behavior, and your feelings. If you sit all day pining away with thoughts of how sad you are at being single, you will not be engaging in building a healthy selfhood. Note these negative thoughts and take action against them. Journaling is a great way to deal with these. You could write them down and turn them into affirmations, or counter them with affirmations. So, if you are thinking "I am going to be single and sad for the rest of my life," you could counter it with an affirmation like "I choose to be single and happy until I am ready to meet my perfect partner."

Calming your thoughts can also help you to create mental space to actually start paying attention to yourself, thinking about what you want and what you need, and enjoying your own company. When you are in a relationship, a lot of your mind is occupied with thoughts of your significant other, who may deserve your time and thoughts, but you also need time and the ability to think about yourself.

Make space upstairs for your life too. By spending more time (and mental space) thinking about yourself, you will also cut down on all the senseless worry you may be engaging in relating to your partner (are they safe, do they love you, are they cheating on you, did they pack lunch, will they still love you when you're old?). Lastly, remember, a cluttered mind can't think logically or clearly, and reasoning distortions may begin to creep in, ruining your progress and happiness.

Chapter 6:

Strategies to Build

Stronger, More Meaningful

Relationships

Building meaningful relationships will for many of us be a lifelong process, and the question arises, "What do healthily attached couples do that is so different from what everyone else is doing?" There are a few significant differences in the approaches favored by healthy couples. However, there are also similar approaches to what everyone else is doing, just differently applied that these couples use.

Key Concepts in Promoting a Secure Attachment

You will be developing your attachment style for the rest of your life as you experience new things, recall old things, meet new people, and deal with the people who started out life with you. This ongoing process can be challenging, and it can often seem like you are falling so short of the mark; however, it's important to remind yourself of these basic tenets:

- **You Are Lovable for You**

One infallible truth you need to recognize and embrace is that you are enough for you. You are lovable enough for you. There is no one's approval and love you need more than your own—yours is what matters. You should not waste time or energy trying to win the approval or love of anyone who doesn't love you for you already.

- **You Are Deserving of Understanding and Compassion**

For some strange reason, we tend to apologize when someone offers us their understanding or compassion when we are feeling down or insufficient. It's almost preprogrammed into us to say, "Oh, I'm sorry for being such a mess." You are allowed to be a mess, and you deserve to have the important people in your life show you understanding and compassion. Even if you have chosen singlehood, you are not alone. Whether you are single or in a relationship, you deserve support.

- **Your Boundaries Should Be Respected**

While a traditional relationship makes an "us" out of you and one other person, you are still entitled to have boundaries. Your personal life, body, and mind does not become open range to your partner. They should respect your boundaries enough not to challenge these. You should have the wisdom to clearly mark what you are confident and happy with sharing and what is private and not up for casual debate. A partner who respects you will respect your boundaries as well.

- **Healthy and Rewarding Communication Is Possible With Someone Who Gets You**

It is the most incredible feeling to speak to someone who gets you. Someone who really understands and gets what you are saying without the words being any different or special than normal. In some cases, that process of being "gotten" happens so seamlessly, you hardly need to speak at all. Some people refer to this as being in sync or on the same wavelength. This is what communication is all about. It is the golden medal at the end of a time of hard work. Building a relationship where you "get" each other is not something that happens over night, but it is so absolutely worth it.

Healing From Trauma Through Emotionally Corrective Relationships

Healing is important, and if we don't address the pain and injuries of the past, we will not be able to engage in meaningful relationships. Engaging with and healing your past trauma is vital to leading a life of empowerment and relationship bliss. Corrective relationships are aimed at helping to support your emotional recovery and healing.

- **Therapy to Face the Past**

A relationship should be a space where growth and recovery can happen. This is what it means when you hear a relationship is a soft place to fall. In a corrective relationship, you find the courage to face past traumas such as abuse, neglect, previous failed relationships, and even current relationships that are on the rocks. If your primary relationship, such as your marriage or life partner, is unable to meet this requirement of being your recovery point, you may have to turn to your therapist or counselor to create a healing or corrective relationship. Having a space to engage with and heal from the past is important to finding your feet in a meaningful relationship.

- **Choosing the Right People for Support**

While your partner is an obvious choice as a support person, you will be well-served to create a support network of people whom you can turn to in a time of crisis. This does not mean people you can go borrow sugar from when you're baking a cake kind of crisis. This is about knowing who to turn to when you need to cry and cry until your emotional rivers run dry. It may be about having someone who can support you to release and laugh with about stressors of your day. It can also be someone whose wisdom and judgment you trust when you don't know which way to go next. Believing your life partner must fulfill all those roles is not only unfair to them but also improbable to be true.

Therefore, you should have a support network that expands beyond your relationship. This does not mean your partner is not enough; instead, it means you know to accept and value all they are *and* turn to others to take unreasonable pressure off your partner. Remember, they are also dealing with their own crisis, past and present, and while they will turn to you, your partner also needs to have their own support network.

- **Healthy Boundaries**

A healthy relationship is built by knowing where you stand. This is achieved by having clear communications and knowing where you are permitted and not permitted in a relationship. Building healthy boundaries is not about saying no; it is about earning respect and understanding from the people in your life who matter most to you. When the lines are drawn within your relationship from the start, you will not have to suffer through the confusion of being pressured when you don't feel comfortable about something.

- **Creating a Conflict Resolution Toolkit**

As with boundaries, when you learn to communicate, you can quickly diminish the impact of conflicting situations and resolve these more peacefully. It is a great feeling to know you and your partner had a difference of opinion or a misunderstanding, but you were able to resolve this in a mature way. Creating a relationship toolkit for conflict resolution may be a great idea. Create some ground rules to stop you from needlessly arguing. This could include rules like:

- Never go to bed still angry.
- If you are not sure, or feel hurt, ask for confirmation first.
- Speak, don't shout.
- Confirm what you heard before you jump to a conclusion.
- If you are unhappy about something, speak about it.
- Listen to your partner too; don't just speak.

Attachment Style Interactions and Their Relationship Challenges

People of different attachment styles interact with each other in dynamic ways and this can become part of the relationship challenges they will face together. Being together despite and in spite of each other.

- **Secure and Secure Attachment**

This is the most secure and successful relationship combination. When both partners in a relationship have a secure attachment style, they will be confident and supportive, caring and considerate, and they will be able to commit and show affection without secretly having concerns the relationship will fail or secretly trying to make it fail.

- **Secure   and   Dismissive-Avoidant Attachment**

When one partner is secure and the other dismissive-avoidant in their attachment styles, this may become a complicated relationship. The secure partner will want to engage in genuine intimacy and trust, but when they try to draw close to their partner, the dismissive-avoidant partner will draw away, avoid them, and even dismiss their efforts. The dismissive-avoidant partner may also be abusive in making light of the other partner's feelings and needs. Emotional intimacy will be complicated. Since the dismissive-avoidant partner is not fully capable of committing to the relationship, this may cause the relationship to break up.

- **Secure and Fearful-Avoidant Attachment**

With one partner being secure in their attachment style and the other fearful-avoidant, many complications can be expected. The secure partner will try to assure their partner of their love and affection, while the fearful-avoidant partner will shelter a secret fear of being single or being alone, yet they want to get out to avoid anticipated pain. This could mean that the partner with the harmful attachment style will intentionally cause conflict, but then cling to the secure attachment partner. They will quickly misread whatever their secure attachment partner says to them, looking for conflict so to speak.

- **Secure and Anxious Attachment**

Should one partner be secure in their attachment styles while the other is anxious avoidant, you have a complicated situation where the insecure partner is constantly trying to get more intimacy and becomes overly demanding for reassurance. They are constantly afraid of being left by the secure partner, who assures them this will not happen, yet over time, they become worn down by the lack of communication and development. Should the relationship end, the partner with an anxious attachment style will quickly jump into the first available relationship, becoming progressively more and more anxious and fearful of being dumped.

- **Dismissive-Avoidant and Dismissive-Avoidant**

When both partners in the relationship have a dismissive-attachment style, the relationship will be cold and hostile. Both partners will lack the initiative to create intimacy and closeness. Communication is also likely to be problematic and somewhat argumentative. Given their withdrawn and dismissive natures, both partners are unlikely to approach a therapist for help either. Problems will not be discussed, and both partners will refrain from spending time together or engaging in joint activities. For children born of such a relationship, their childhood will be filled with cold arguments between their parents, a lack of affection, and a slow response to their needs.

- **Dismissive-Avoidant and Fearful-Avoidant Attachment**

This type of relationship will be a clear case of abuser and victim. The dismissive-avoidant partner will be aggressive to and manipulative of their fearful-avoidant partner who will cower and be unable to stand up for themselves. The relationship will not be likely to survive for long, and the fearful-avoidant partner will either self-isolate themselves within the relationship or they will bail on the relationship.

- **Dismissive-Avoidant and Anxious Attachment**

When one partner is a dismissive-avoidant and the other is anxious behavior styled, you will have a situation where the dismissive-avoidant partner will be dominating towards the anxious behavior-styled partner. Abuse may be present, often spilling over onto the children of such a relationship. The home of the relationship will be a place of nervous tension, and the dismissive-avoidant partner will be unable to tolerate any form of criticism, responding to it with aggression. As a result, the anxious partner will become even more anxious, and though they want to leave, they will not do so as that would mean being on their own, which they can't handle.

- **Anxious and Fearful-Avoidant Attachment**

With a relationship made up of an anxious and a fearful-avoidant styled partnership, there will be less violence, but both partners will display negative characteristics such as jealousy, fear, anxiety, and lack intimacy. While the anxious partner will need assurances, their fearful-avoidant partner will be unable to provide these as they already believe the worst will happen. This will, in turn, make the anxious partner more anxious, causing the fearful-avoidant partner to become even more terrified and withdraw even more. This is a worst case-scenario of two partners bringing out the worst in each other.

- **Anxious and Anxious Attachment**

While a relationship with two partners who are both anxious in their attachment styles may seem like a place where mutual anxiety could lead to understanding, this is not the case. While both partners need assurance, they don't have the confidence to meet this need for each other, which will again see an escalation of even more anxiety and feelings of inadequacy in the relationship. This form of relationship is also quite rare as anxious styled people tend to be attracted to either secure or dismissive-avoidant styled partners who project confidence or dominate them into submission.

- **Fearful-Avoidant and Fearful-Avoidant Attachment**

In a relationship where both partners have fearful-avoidant style approaches to behavior, there may be a substantial lack of communication. Both partners will be afraid of the relationship failing, and both will avoid doing anything about that. They will lack commitment and confidence, and as a result, they may engage in extramarital relationships when pressured to do so. This is often not based on any sexual needs being met but more on avoiding committing to the relationship. Yet, when their partner discovers the infidelity, they may become fearful of the relationship ending.

While being in a relationship with someone who is not secure in their attachment style can be difficult, it can work out when both partners are there to support each other and look on the upside and not on the downside.

Exercises to Strengthen Your Relationship

It is possible to strengthen your relationship with someone whom you may have become disillusioned with. After all, there was something that attracted you to them in the beginning, and it was not what is now pushing you away.

- **List Exercise**

Try this exercise to strengthen your relationship (Vilhauer, 2017). It could possibly give you the inspiration to fight to save your relationship:

Use Your Journal

Sit comfortably somewhere quiet, close your eyes, and begin to think back to when you first met. Can you recall what your partner was like? What was it that attracted you to them in the beginning? There was something you felt when you knew they were coming over, or you were going somewhere with them—write it down now.

List

In your journal, create a list with all of the best qualities your partner had when you were dating that attracted you most to them. It could be how they were considerate of your comfort, how they smiled when you complimented them, or how they were funny. Try to make your list as detailed as possible.

Add to It

Every day, when you are getting ready for bed, use your journal and the list you created to add three new points you appreciate about your partner today. It does not have to be big things like them buying you a car. It can also be something small like smiling at you, or how they made you coffee to go because you were running late for work.

Read It

The following morning, take some time as you get up to read your list and reflect on it, recalling more precious and meaningful moments as you ponder on this little list.

Grow for 30 Days

Faithfully keep adding three things to your list about your partner *every* day. After 30 days, there will be a much less negative impression about your partner in your heart and mind. You may find the list growing much bigger than you had anticipated. Where it may take you three hours to write down the three things on the second day, you may find you are burning to write down three things by day 20. It will also make you much more observant of the good things about your partner and about your relationship with that person.

- **Learn Something New**

Communication and learning is what keeps a relationship interesting and novel. Try spending some time every night learning something new about your partner. Even though you may have been together for five years or fifty years, you don't know everything about each other yet. So, open the avenues of communication by finding out:

Something funny

Something embarrassing or awkward

Something they love

Something they hate

A random childhood story

If you are not sure about where to start, paging through some childhood photo albums may be helpful. If your partner has had a traumatic childhood, you may need to proceed carefully, gently guiding them to recall the best memories and not dwell on painful past events.

- **Ask Questions**

Learning about your partner can also be driven by questions that may be difficult to answer. Be open about this, encourage them to ask freely, and be prepared to answer truthfully. Use some time over coffee or while getting ready for bed. On pieces of paper, write down some difficult questions you have never asked each other. It may be a good idea to place the questions into a jar and select one every night to both answer to each other. This could become part of your pillow-talk routine. Questions could include:

Name your biggest fear and explain.

Tell me about your biggest dream that still hasn't come true.

What is your biggest regret in life?

Share your fondest childhood memory.

Who is your hero and why?

If you could change one thing in your life, what is it and why?

- **Soul Gazing**

Even if you have been in your relationship for years, you may not be familiar with your partner's soul, and this can be a daunting yet important aspect of them to meet. While the eyes are said to be the windows of the soul, we so rarely gaze into our partner's eyes with any lasting intensity. So, try this exercise in soul gazing:

Sit comfortably with your knees touching and look into each other's eyes. Keep your eyes focused but soft, not trying to intimidate or judge with your look. Instead, simply look with a steady visual presence into your partner's eyes. Don't break eye contact, but you may blink. However, look into their eyes as if they are the only person on earth. This is not a contest; it isn't about who looks away first and losing. Instead, you may find yourself realizing aspects about your partner you had not previously known. You may see their and your vulnerabilities, which creates trust and companionship.

- **Attentive Listening**

How often have you longed to speak to your partner, to unburden your mind without them interrupting or offering advice or telling you off or doing anything other than listening to you with complete attention? This exercise is precisely about this, and you can and should use a timer set to five minutes to ensure both partners get their fair share of listening and talking time.

When it is your turn to speak, simply let yourself ramble on about what has been on your mind. It does not have to be anything serious or hugely deep, although you may find your deepest thoughts flowing out before you know it. Whatever you or your partner says, the listener should simply remain quietly listening. Do not ask questions, don't offer suggestions, and don't offer encouraging sounds like "oh," "ah," or "hmm." Instead, just listen, making gentle eye contact or being physically close. When the timer sounds, change positions with the listener becoming talking and vice versa.

- **Spend Some Time on Worksheets for Couples**

The internet abounds with free downloadable worksheets to help couples connect and improve their communication skills. Two excellent examples of this is the *About Your Partner Worksheet,* which is designed to help you discover things about your partner and also show how much you know about your partner (or don't). This worksheet focuses on six subcategories ranging from questions about fun and games to your feelings and careers.

Another useful worksheet is the *Good Qualities Worksheet,* which is designed to help you remember positive points about your partner with guided questions. These worksheets and many others are available from Positive Psychology at https://positivepsychology.com/couples-therapy-worksheets-activities/ and though they may not be a quick fix for your relationship problems, they can breathe new life into your relationship and help you find common ground as well as improving your communication skills.

Chapter 7:

Long-Term Relationship

Happiness: What's the

Secret?

Image 10: Karan Mandre on Unsplash. The expression "you can't make an omelet without breaking a few eggs" may seem to apply to the whole messy business of dating and finding your perfect partner. You may even have broken several dozen and still

not found what you need to make you happy and create a meaningful and successful relationship. Perhaps you have found your partner, but you fear losing them, and you wish there were a way to keep your heart fires burning strong. So, what is the secret to long-term relationship bliss?

A relationship requires skills you may not have been magically born with. But don't fret; you can develop them with dedication and an openness to learning. There are several skills that will serve you well in creating and maintaining a long-term relationship. Here are some of the most important ones:

Your Emotional Intelligence

Being in command of your emotions, you can make decisions based not only on an involuntary reaction but also on your reaction to others and with your own internal environment. Having an evolved emotional intelligence (EQ) will lead to you being able to know what you feel and why you feel it. You will also be able to interpret how other people are feeling. You are a master of empathy. However, sadly, EQ is not necessarily something you are born with, though we all have it in differing degrees. Practicing it will certainly improve it, but how do you polish up this skill that can have a huge impact on your relationship and maintain your connected bliss? Golhar (2018) has suggestions to try:

- **Be Assertive in Your Communications**

Being assertive is not being aggressive. When you have a well-developed EQ, you know the difference. Practice communicating clearly but respectfully.

- **Respond, Don't React**

When tempers run high, we are all inclined to respond in haste and in anger. Our emotions can be a hot pot of trauma, and if we don't take control of this, we spill words we can't ever take back. When you are emotionally mature, you learn to think before you speak and before you act. Reacting is based on emotions, such as running when you hear a gunshot because you are afraid. Thinking will help you develop and maintain integrity within your relationship.

- **Listen**

Often, the death of a relationship is due to a misunderstanding, which could have been prevented if you had simply listened and gotten clarity before reacting. Listening before you react or before you allow your emotions to race off will help you communicate better and avoid confusion and misunderstandings.

- **Self-Motivate and Be Positive**

Be your own cheerleader. The world is not always likely to cheer you on, so it's up to you to motivate yourself and find positive energy to push on through with. In a relationship, we often demand our partner to be our supporter or fan, neglecting that they have their own draining issues to deal with. By self-motivating and building a positive mindset, you will be able to value your partner so much more and not just because they make you feel good. When you are positive, you will also have a different life outlook that will open up your energy for the day ahead. You will be less grumpy and more accessible to your partner too.

- **Embrace Criticism**

None of us are perfect. Being mature enough to embrace this, you will seek to engage in self-improvement, and you will not be upset by constructive criticism. Since you are then looking to improve your skills, you will be much more observant about yourself and the world around you. People will become signboards to you, advertising what they are thinking and feeling, which will help you make better decisions. When you get it wrong, you need to choose not to react in a negative or defensive way. Instead, you can use this as feedback to help you improve and develop more, constantly becoming a better version of yourself.

- **Empathize but Lead**

Feeling bad for someone who is in crisis is not a weakness. It is strength to be able to see what someone is going through and feel an emotional connection to them. This does not mean you (should) feel sorry for them. Instead, it is about understanding what they are going through. This understanding will help you to be a better partner.

When someone is in despair, you can help ease their burdens by leading. While you understand what they are going through, you need to be strong and lead until they are able to get on their feet. Sitting there crying with them will not avail either of you of anything.

- **Remain Accessible and Social**

While we all want to be with someone whom we can drop all of our guards with, letting our hair down and not being as guarded with our emotions, we still need to consider the impact of this emotional rawness on our partners. They may not be as comfortable with seeing the unrestrained us. Having some social skills and knowing that having a bad day is not an excuse for shouting at our partner will help us remain accessible. In addition, emotionally intelligent people know they should communicate with their partners especially. Saying to your partner that you had a bad work day and need 15 minutes of quiet time before you join them to prepare dinner is being mature. It shows a heightened EQ. Your partner will thank you for being up front and honest, avoiding later misunderstandings.

Strengthen Your Communication Skills

Communication is one of the most vital relationship skills, and when you are able to do it effectively, you will be assured of being understood and understanding your partner correctly. Much of the conflict and trauma in relationships are from misunderstandings and an inability to communicate effectively. When you want something, you should be able to ask for it clearly and negotiate to get it without hurting or harming your partner. Likewise, as a responsible partner, you need to be able to listen to and understand your partner's needs, being careful to ask when you are not sure. To communicate better, consider the following carefully:

- **Honesty As Much As Possible**

Complete honesty is not always possible or advisable. When your partner asks if their body is getting old, you may need to avoid that cut-like-a-knife honesty of telling them they are getting old to their face. However, when your partner asks your opinion about something meaningful in the relationship, or if you need to tell them how you feel about something, you need to be honest and explain. Vague statements like, "I'm not going to the park because I don't like it" will not help communication much. However, if you explain honestly that you don't like the park because you feel uncomfortable with so many people you don't know around you, it will help your partner understand without mistakenly thinking it is about them.

Deliberately lying to your partner is unacceptable. Saying one thing and not sticking to it will only make you seem unreliable, and this is what honesty means. It boils down to the old adage of "Your word is your bond." Honesty can be a beautiful thing as it assures your partner, and they always know where they stand with you. They will also be more inclined to ask your opinion on matters then. However, don't respond in ways that seem like honesty but are actually malicious comments. Telling your overweight partner they no longer turn you on is not honesty. You could rather express this as being concerned for their health.

- **Apologize When You've Been Wrong**

We are often so set on winning that we don't realize when we argue with our partner we are actually both losing. Many times, we argue to hide that we have actually been wrong. Own up to your flaws and mistakes. There is nothing more sexy than someone who apologizes with complete honesty when they were mistaken or acted incorrectly. You will find your partner trusts you all the more when you are mature enough to tell them you were wrong and you are sorry. This is not about begging. It is about admitting your flaws and asking for forgiveness when your words or deeds have wronged your partner as a result.

When you apologize, mean it. So often people say "I'm sorry," but they hardly know what those words mean. It's become a preprogrammed response that we use like a "get out of jail free" card. Apologizing means admitting honestly you have been wrong, asking for the other person's forgiveness, and fully intending not to repeat this harmful behavior you did again. Asking for forgiveness when you had an extramarital affair, but still have your fling on the side, is not a real apology. Know the difference. One type of apology will allow your relationship to grow through difficult times, while the other will most certainly lead to its death.

- **Resolve Conflict Calmly**

Shouting and arguing in a relationship will not create a happy relationship. While you have probably heard that arguing is great for the make-up sex after, this will not help to strengthen your relationship. Instead, you should work towards facing conflict as two mature adults who are able to calmly talk about their conflict and find a way to resolve this without resorting to screaming, name calling, or haranguing.

- **Walk in Your Partner's Shoes**

We each have our own truth, our own version of reality. While you might see something a certain way, your partner may see it differently. Their life view is determined by their experiences and unique personality. When you know them really well, you will be able to consider a situation from their point of view. This is the proverbial version of walking in their shoes. It is great for your relationship as it ensures you can really consider your partner's needs and anticipate how they would react to a certain situation. This becomes a really important skill when you are arguing with or angry at your partner. It's easy to remain angry when you simply believe the other person is the bad guy. However, when you can begin to see why they did something or said something, you can more readily forgive them or let go of your anger. Without this understanding, you will likely turn to resentment instead.

• Question, Don't Assume

"Assumptions are the mother of all..." Well, we all know how that ends. Sadly, it is true. When we assume something, we are acting on what we believe we know. We put our thinking over the truth, and that does not end well. Here are a few cases of assumptions ending badly:

Your husband does not listen to what you are saying, so you assume he is not interested and feel hurt by him.

Your wife is not interested in being intimate tonight, so you assume she has found something on the side.

In both these cases, your thinking may be faulty. There are other reasons why people may be distracted or unwilling. Your husband may be busy watching a business report on the news that will affect your family's investments. Your wife may be tired after a long day, or she may be worrying about a lump in her breast and be unsure of how to tell you about it.

To avoid making assumptions and engaging in flawed reasoning, you should ask. Tap your husband on the shoulder and ask why he is not listening and if something is wrong. Hold your wife and ask her if something is wrong that she is not interested in having sex tonight. Be patient and encouraging with your partner. Remember, they may need some coaxing to admit to what is really bothering them. But ask, don't assume.

- **Take a Break When You're Angry**

Anger is one of our most powerful emotions, and often, it shows us when something is wrong. However, it can also be incredibly destructive within a relationship. As a golden rule: don't speak to your partner when you are angry. Instead, call a time-out. Spend some time alone until you can let go of your anger and speak to your partner calmly. In addition, respect your partner's need to decompress their anger before they speak to you. Don't pressure them into an argument either.

Healing Your Trauma and Moving Towards Secure Attachment

While most of us are not secure in our attachment style, we can improve on our behavior styles. This is not an overnight process; however, you can seriously improve your relationship by dealing with your past traumas and making your partner part of the healing process. Remember, when you enter a relationship with unresolved past traumas, you make your pain their pain. Your partner becomes a part of the process; don't shut them out.

- **Share Your Fear and Pain**

Sharing is caring. This is a simple truth. When you share with your partner, you enable them to care about you, and this is nowhere more true in your relationship than when you share your fear and pain with them. Your partner does not expect you to be Mr. or Mrs. Perfect, so don't try to be. Trust them enough to be vulnerable and open up. This will help them understand you and help you heal.

- **Include Them**

While the past traumas are yours to heal from, your partner can help. They want to help. It will bring an additional closeness in your relationship. So, include them. Let them go with you to therapy sessions and attend couple's therapy sessions together. Build stronger bonds by including and sharing.

- **Let Go**

Your partner married or chose to be in a relationship with you. They didn't necessarily sign up for marrying your pain or the past trauma. When you do not deal with this trauma, you are effectively making it a third party to your relationship. Your partner didn't sign up for a threesome. At some point, you need to let go of the past and release your pain or trauma. Your partner can help you, but only up to a point. You need to let go.

- **Create Proactive Co-Habits**

When dealing with past traumas, you need to build supporting habits with your partner. Making healthy routines to replace the pain or trauma of your past will help you move on and move more towards your partner. Go for walks together when you are feeling stressed, or turn off the TV and snuggle on the sofa when you are feeling lonely or inadequate. Habits of support with your partner will increase your positive energies and help you release the burden of your past.

- **Kick Back Together**

Working on your past is hard. It can be emotionally and physically draining, and you need a time-out from this. Having a partner whom you can kick back with and just be fun and silly with will help you be more relaxed and balance the negative you are dealing with internally. Watch a movie, dance like teenagers to the latest dance tracks in your living room, bake cookies together and decorate them like angry birds. Find something to do that releases your frustrations in a fun and healthy way.

- **Be Kind When You Experience Darkness**

No matter how much effort you put in to resolve your past trauma, there will be days when you slip backwards in the process. You may wake up and feel totally overwhelmed, or you may see something that reminds you of the pain and trauma anew. This is when you need to be kind to yourself and your partner. Don't lash out because you are suddenly hurting. Communicate about how you are feeling and what is happening.

Compromise

A relationship is about give and take. It is very much a business interaction. Both partners need to share equal benefit or it does not work. This means you need to compromise to maintain a balance. BOTH partners compromise, not one partner giving and the other constantly taking. This is how you do it:

- **Meet in the Middle**

Compromise means meeting each other in the middle. You need to give equally, take equally, and agree on who gives when and how much. Without being thoughtful towards your partner, you can quickly become a bully who always takes from their partner. This will lead to resentment.

- **Introduce Healthy Compromise**

When you change to meet the needs of both parties in the relationship, this is compromise. It is healthy when it benefits both of you. By entering a give-and-take discussion as part of daily life, you will easily and elegantly begin doing it in the relationship.

- **Know Your Boundaries**

There are some things we will not be happy to let go of or compromise on. These are your boundaries, and you should communicate them clearly to your partner. If you are an avid cyclist, and your partner wants you to stop doing this to spend more time with them, you need to be clear in communicating how this is crossing a boundary you are not willing to break. Rather compromise with your partner, cycling when they are at work or when they have an afternoon nap. Being asked to give it up completely will be a breach of boundaries your partner knew existed and it is not a mutually beneficial compromise.

Privacy and Personal Time

While we are often working on the creation of an "us" within the relationship, we should not lose sight that we are also two individual and unique people within that "us." When you are securely attached, you do not need to spend every waking moment together. You are then confident enough to give each other some alone time. We all need time to be on our own or engage in our own hobbies and do things that may be more for our pleasure and not necessarily interesting to our partner.

You do not have to share all your friends, and it is impractical and illogical to think you will both have the same friends. You have needs your partner may not be able to meet. These could include some bro-time with your buddies or some girl-time with your sisters. Your securely attached partner will respect this.

Be Open and Honest About Difficult Questions

Communication is easy when it comes to the easy stuff, but it really matters when you discuss the less common or difficult topics. Speaking to your partner about things like sex, money, time, chores, to parent or not, and even where to live can be difficult. However, you can't shut your eyes and refuse to discuss these topics, or they will become issues in your relationship. Here are some useful suggestions for sensitive topics and how to discuss them:

- **Fair Division of Chores**

In a modern relationship, the division of chores may not necessarily work when you are not functioning in a purely traditional role. Expecting the woman to take care of housework is not practical when she is also earning money. Insisting the man deals with all "manly issues" such as plumbing and fixing is also not feasible. This will require discussion and compromise.

Today, it is quite natural to find men participating in and doing their share of the household chores. While they may not have acquired the skills to deal with all "manly chores" and the woman may not be a skilled "homemaker" who sews, cooks, and cleans, there needs to be a middle ground. Agree on what will be outsourced, what will be shared equally, and what is within one partner's particular skills set. Do not assume someone *must* do something.

- **Sex and Intimacy**

There is a lot of conflict in relationships that originate from sex and intimacy. We all have our own preferences, and wanting someone else to perform what and when we want is not healthy. Openly communicating what you like and don't like will help to find a way to satisfy and meet the needs of both partners. Again, this is a give and take too. While you may not be particularly turned on by something, your partner may find it very satisfying, and you should discuss this, finding a solution that suits both of you.

It is easy to say that both partners should initiate sex and intimacy; however, this is not always the reality of your relationship. Each of us have our own inhibitions and past experiences that influence how we behave and what we feel comfortable doing. Don't hide from this. Talk about it and be supportive of each other.

- **Finances**

Traditionally, the man has been the partner who dealt with financial decisions. However, with changing times, and with the woman also earning money (sometimes even earning more than the man), this needs some discussion. You should openly discuss your investment goals, what to do with your monthly expenses, who pays for what, and importantly, you should ensure each partner has their own money they do not need to account for.

Remember, you are individuals within the "us." If you want to buy new make-up or a Harley Davidson (and if there is money available after your monthly expenses), then you should be allowed to do so without your partner scolding you about it like a child. Again, consider your partner, and remember, an equal division of expenses only works when you earn an equal income.

- **Your Joint Future**

Making plans for your future needs to include both parties. When you plan where you see yourselves in the near, middle, and far future, you should include your partner. Discuss your relationship goals, how you plan on dealing with complications such as ill-health, loss of income, the introduction of external pressures, and conflict resolution strategies. While you can't plan for every eventuality, you should at least talk about it.

• Becoming Parents or Not

Deciding whether you will have children is not a simple choice today. Women have the right to decide what happens to their bodies, as do men. Discuss if, when, and how you will decide to have children. Your discussion might include whether you perhaps want to rather adopt or foster children. Your partner should support your decision, and you should be open and communicative about your reasons for your decision. Importantly, don't fall into the trap of believing children are the cement of a relationship. If your relationship is already not working well, adding children to the mix will not end well.

Spontaneity and Doing Fun Things Together

Relationships are a lot of work, and some of it is really serious. This can quickly suck the life out of your companionship. Remember, you probably started off enjoying each other's company. This should not stop. So, make time to do fun activities together where you can just be two people having a good time. Do fun stuff together and build common interests.

If you are so bound up in your chores and work and planning how to save or maintain your relationship, then you might want to plan for fun. Writing down some crazy (but doable ideas) on scraps of paper, stick them in a jar. Every week you take turns to draw one scrap of paper. Set aside some time over a weekend to go do this activity. Some ideas could include:

- Going go-karting
- Ice-skating
- Watching a movie
- Dancing at the local club
- Going on an adventure at the paintball club
- Having a fancy dress party at home
- Taking a mini road trip
- Planning a scavenger hunt around your home or neighborhood

The Importance of Touch and Physical Intimacy

Relationships have a physical component, and we can easily forget this as we age and when we become busy with life. Even when you are entering the later part of your life, you can still benefit from touch and physical intimacy. Holding and being held is a gift to your bodies. Physical touch activates feel-good endorphins that help you connect and deal with stress. Explore where you and your partner enjoy being touched and how.

When you are younger, this may also improve your sex-life, but it is essential to touch and support each other physically. This will meet your need for intimacy and companionship for your body. Couples who regularly touch each other and practice physical intimacy (not sex) have less likelihood of infidelity within the couple. So, touch is important when building a long-term relationship.

Don't Try to Change Each Other, Respect Your Differences

There was a joke going around a few years ago, where it is said that during the wedding ceremony, women who walked down the aisle next to their husband would think, "Aisle, alter him." You marry someone for who they are. You enter a relationship with someone based on who they are. It is not up to you to alter them or make them into who you want.

Relationships are most successful when you can accept your partner, be respectful of your differences, and be there in a supportive capacity to the life changes your partner chooses to engage in. You may be part of their healing journey, but you are not there to fix them. Your partner is not a broken-down car you can fix up and impress everyone with. They are real humans too, and they deserve your love and respect.

Cultivate Patience and Respect

Your partner is not perfect; nor are you. Having a little patience with each other will help you to develop together into a successful unit of respect and support. There may be small things that niggle at your patience. Evaluate these calmly and don't become angry over petty things. We all have boiling points when we have just had enough, but we should deal with this as a loving partnership. Venting on social media or to a friend will not only do irreparable damage to your partnership, but it will lessen you as a person. Respect each other enough to deal with all things inside your relationship, and if you can't, then approach a relationship professional.

Know When It's Time to Get Out

You can and should try your best for your relationship. However, sometimes your attachment styles are simply not compatible, and when your partner is not willing to put in the work you are, it ends up being a case of leading a horse to water and not being able to make them drink. This is the point where you need to consider whether you should end the relationship or not.

- **Recognize Signs**

If you already have a secure attachment style, you may discover your relationship is not working, nor is it meeting your needs. Being responsible and caring, you will have tried to build on the relationship deficit with your partner, but sometimes, this is not enough, or they are not willing to show the same commitment as you. This is not a sign of failure on your part. It is simply an indication of signs that the relationship can't be made to work. Incompatibility is more common than many people realize, and sticking together can be harmful to all parties involved, especially if there are children involved.

- **The Best Decision**

It sounds really tragic to say you can end a relationship. However, this need not be a death or complete severing of ties. After all, you have a history together, and unless you have been in an abusive relationship, you can redefine the relationship to become platonic and not romantic. There are many instances of couples who divorced and became good friends after, even including their new partners or spouses in their friendships. In the end, being miserable together is not healthy for either party involved in a relationship. Separating or ending the relationship is the only viable and responsible option then.

- **Irreparable Damage**

When you evaluate your relationship, you will quickly be able to identify if the damage has been irreparable, or if there is still hope to repair misunderstandings and miscommunications. Irreparable damage to your relationship could include trust that is broken, there is no attraction of connection between you and your partner, communication is impossible or one-sided, you constantly feel unhappy and bad in the relationship, and if you have developed a loathing or contempt for your partner. When your partner is continually abusive, you also owe it to yourself to walk away. If you find yourself in any of these irreparable situations, you know it is time to leave; the damage is done and there is no way to save an un-savable situation.

- **Walking Out**

When you have made your decision to leave, you should do so in a responsible and mature manner. Now is not the time to be vindictive or immature about your relationship. Discuss it clearly with your partner, drawing a line where intimacy will end (if it hasn't already), and resolve the division of material and financial assets in an amicable manner. Though you are no longer together, there is no reason to be enemies. When there are children involved, you have a responsibility to keep channels of communication open to their other parent.

Conclusion

"Our minds influence the key activity of the brain, which then influences everything; perception, cognition, thoughts and feelings, personal relationships; they're all a projection of you."

~ Deepak Chopra

We are each of us unique projections of the summation of experiences in our minds. What has happened to us has shaped us and formed us into who we are and how we behave. This not only influences how we act, but also how we react to the people around us. In relationships, this can create chaos or harmony.

By knowing your attachment style, you can be aware of your flaws and strong points, and with a little guidance, you can also improve the chances of finding and keeping love. Your behavior is a result of your mind and your emotions warring over control. When you begin to take responsibility for both these, you can become rational instead of reactional. However, this is a battle with yourself, and though we often want to blame others for our flaws, we are solely responsible for who we are.

Sharing ourselves within the confines of a relationship begins with the relationship with yourself. You have the power to make yourself happy, to meet your needs, and to find satisfaction in your own company. When you are ready, confident, and secure in who you are and how to interact with the world, you are most suited to entering a relationship, if you choose to.

Thinking, Feeling, and Doing

When you have formed a secure attachment style, you are able to manage conflict in your relationships, give freely, and love completely. You do not jump to conclusions or impose your will. The Ancient Delphic maxim of "know thyself" has never been more valid than here. When you have self-awareness, you are more geared to being a responsible and valuable partner for your right partner regardless of the life stage you are at.

Finding, Fixing, and Healing

When you are already in a complicated relationship, you can engage in several therapeutic approaches to help you find yourself within the relationship. Great value can be gleaned from consulting with an EFFT therapist to help you deal with emotion-based thinking in your relationship with your partner and in your relationship with yourself. Cognitive behavior therapy is a great asset to anyone wanting to build up their own skills in thinking clearly and acting mindfully. Self-betterment and the improvement of your relationships is always a worthy cause and one you should make time for and commit to.

Whether you are single or in a relationship, you can learn the skills to find your and your relationship challenges and traumas, fix them, and heal them. A relationship with another person is a constant investment of time, effort, and care. When you do it right, and when your partner is there for the journey with you, your relationship will gift you with love, contentment, belonging, and happiness.

References

Ackerman, C. E. (2020a). *What is Attachment Theory? Bowlby's 4 Stages Explained.* Positive Psychology. https://positivepsychology.com/attachment-theory/

Ackerman, C. E. (2020b). *Emotion Focused Therapy: Understanding Emotions to Improve Relationships.* Positive Psychology. https://positivepsychology.com/emotion-focused-therapy/

Ackerman, C. E. (2020c). *25 CBT Techniques and Worksheets for Cognitive Behavioral Therapy.* Positive psychology. https://positivepsychology.com/cbt-cognitive-behavioral-therapy-techniques-worksheets/

Brenner, G. H. (2018). *The Art and Psychology of Being Single.* Psychology Today. https://www.psychologytoday.com/za/blog/experimentations/201808/the-art-and-psychology-being-single

Cherry, K. (2020). *The Different Types of Attachment Styles.* Very Well Mind. https://www.verywellmind.com/attachment-styles-2795344

Chopra, D. (n.d.). *Personal Relationships Quotes*. Brainy Quote.
https://www.brainyquote.com/quotes/deepak_chopra_599977?src=t_personal_relationships

Church, D. (2017). *American Psychological Association Standards and EFT*. EFT Universe. https://www.eftuniverse.com/building-a-thriving-practice/american-psychological-association-standards-and-eft

Golhar, A. (2018). *10 Ways to Increase Your Emotional Intelligence*. Inc. https://www.inc.com/young-entrepreneur-council/10-ways-to-increase-your-emotional-intelligence.html

Helpguide. (n.d.). *Therapy for Anxiety Disorders*. https://www.helpguide.org/articles/anxiety/therapy-for-anxiety-disorders.htm#~:text=Cognitive%20behavioral%20therapy%20(CBT)%20for%20anxiety&text=Research%20has%20shown%20it%20to,at%20the%20world%20and%20ourselves.

Johnson, S. M. (2009). Attachment Theory and Emotionally Focused Therapy for Individuals and Couples. *Attachment Theory and Research in Clinical Work with Adults*. http://www.creatingconnections.nl/assets/files/Sue%20Johnson%20ObegiCh16.pdf

Levine, L. & Heller, R. S. F. (2010). *Deciphering Your Own Attachment Style*. Attached.

https://www.attachedthebook.com/wordpress/compatibility-quiz/?step=1

Reach Out. (n.d.). *Teach Your Teenager Coping Skills for Fellbeing.* Reach Out. https://parents.au.reachout.com/skills-to-build/wellbeing/things-to-try-coping-skills-and-resilience/teach-your-teenager-coping-skills-for-wellbeing

Reese, C. (2007). Childhood Attachment. *British Journal of General Practice,* 57(544): 920–922. https://doi.org/10.3399/096016407782317955

Stavrianopoulos, K. (2019). *Emotionally Focused Family Therapy: Rebuilding Family Bonds.* Intechopen. https://www.intechopen.com/books/family-therapy-new-intervention-programs-and-researches/emotionally-focused-family-therapy-rebuilding-family-bonds

Vilhauer, J. (2017). *This One Exercise Can Improve Your Relationship Today.* Psychology Today. https://www.psychologytoday.com/us/blog/living-forward/201710/one-exercise-can-improve-your-relationship-today

West-Olatunji, C. A., Wolfgang, J. D. & Frazier, K. N. (2019). *Interventions for attachment and traumatic stress issues in young children.* Counseling Today. https://ct.counseling.org/2019/04/interventions-for-attachment-and-traumatic-stress-issues-in-young-children/

Whitbourne, S. K. (2012). *The 12 Ties that Bind Long-Term Relationships.* Psychology Today. https://www.psychologytoday.com/za/blog/fu lfillment-any-age/201206/the-12-ties-bind-long-term-relationships

Whitbourne, S. K. (2013). *What Rising Divorce Rates in Midlife Mean for You.* Psychology Today. https://www.psychologytoday.com/za/blog/fu lfillment-any-age/201311/what-rising-divorce-rates-in-midlife-mean-you

Yerkovich, M. & Yerkovich K. (n.d.). *What is a Love Style?* How We Love. https://howwelove.com/love-styles/

Image References

Image 1: Geralt on Pixabay. https://pixabay.com/illustrations/woman-face-photomontage-faces-1594710/

Image 2: Kelly Sikkema on Unsplash. https://unsplash.com/photos/XX2WTbLr3r8

Image 3: mohamed_hassan on pixabay. https://pixabay.com/vectors/silhouette-relationship-conflict-3141264/

Image 4: maz-Alph from Pixabay. https://pixabay.com/vectors/stage-of-life-childhood-life-1287959/

Image 5: sweetlouise on pixaybay. https://pixabay.com/photos/friendship-brotherhood-love-freedom-2156171/

Image 6: Julie Rose from Pixabay. https://pixabay.com/photos/couple-romantic-together-vintage-5302344/

Image 7: Rostyslav Savchyn on Unsplash. https://unsplash.com/photos/E2zvqyY5zUY

Image 8: Hannah Olinger on Unsplash. https://unsplash.com/photos/8eSrC43qdro

Image   9:   Priscilla   Du   Preez   on   Unsplash.
https://unsplash.com/photos/5eO8WdwszAQ

Image   10:   Karan   Mandre   on   Unsplash.
https://unsplash.com/photos/FUYSmgif7c8